T0193266

"Gramma... Gramma... Gramma..."

The Lord's Lessons from Little Lambs

JEANNIE K. HOLM

WESTBOW
PRESS®
A DIVISION OF THOMAS NELSON
& ZONDERVAN

This book is a work of non-fiction. Unless otherwise noted, the author and the publisher make no explicit guarantees as to the accuracy of the information contained in this book and in some cases, names of people and places have been altered to protect their privacy.

WestBow Press books may be ordered through booksellers or by contacting:

WestBow Press
A Division of Thomas Nelson & Zondervan
1663 Liberty Drive
Bloomington, IN 47403
www.westbowpress.com
844-714-3454

Scripture quotations marked NIV are taken from The Holy Bible, New International Version®, NIV® Copyright © 1973, 1978, 1984, 2011 by Biblica, Inc.® Used by permission. All rights reserved worldwide.

Scripture quotations marked KJV are taken from the King James Version.

Scripture quotations marked ESV taken from The Holy Bible, English Standard Version® (ESV®), Copyright © 2001 by Crossway, a publishing ministry of Good News Publishers. All rights reserved.

ISBN: 978-1-6642-7538-6 (sc)
ISBN: 978-1-6642-7539-3 (hc)
ISBN: 978-1-6642-7537-9 (e)

Library of Congress Control Number: 2022915035

Print information available on the last page.

WestBow Press rev. date: 08/17/2022

†

THERE IS A SAYING THAT goes as follows: if we don't teach our children to follow Jesus, the world will teach them not to.

I have taken that to heart. I take every opportunity to talk *about* the Lord to my grandchildren. On the other hand, I also take every opportunity to talk *to* the Lord about my grandchildren. Deuteronomy 11:13, 18–19, says, "So if you faithfully obey the commands, I am giving you today—to love your God and serve him with all your heart and with all your soul … Fix these words of mine in your hearts and minds; tie them as symbols on your hands and bind them on your foreheads. Teach them to your children, talking about them when you sit at home and when you walk along the road, when you lie down and when you get up" (NIV).

✝

I BELIEVE THERE IS NO greater legacy to leave behind at the end of my life than to have shared my love for the Lord and to instill the importance of not only reading but memorizing scripture, absorbing the Word of God, and spending time with Him daily.

When we apply His Word to our lives, we can be a living witness of God's love, a life always striving to submit and surrender to God's will. Then, as in everything, taking to heart the words in 1 Thessalonians 5:17, "Pray without ceasing" (KJV).

In June 1974, I married my high school sweetheart, Richard (Bucky) Holm. We purchased my grandparents' home, which was only two blocks from where I grew up. I liked living close to my parents and siblings. I was the first one to leave home.

In the spring of the following year, we decided to do a little remodeling. We were young newlyweds. We woke up one Saturday morning and decided to tear out a wall in our main floor that was between the living room and the only downstairs bedroom. Both rooms were small. We were very happy to have a bigger living room, and, after all, we had two bedrooms upstairs. It was only the two of us, so that was all we really needed.

Now fast-forward a few years. We not only had been blessed with a daughter, Lisa, and three boys, Joe, Nick, and Tony, but we were expecting our fifth child. You are right; those two bedrooms were not enough room for all of us.

My husband and I looked into taking out a loan to add on to our much too small house. After talking to the bank, we realized we also had too small of a budget to add on. We had trusted in the Lord for the provision of our family. We both felt strongly that I was supposed to stay at home to raise our children. We were living on one income, and that would not change. We called on Him, asking for help in what seemed to be an impossible situation. But Romans 8:28 says, "And we know that in all things God works for the good of those who love Him, who have been called according to His purpose" (NIV).

In May of that year, I had been praying about our house situation. I was about five months into my pregnancy, and the reality of our tiny house was weighing on me. As I prayed that day, a peace came over me. It was so unbelievable, but I felt for certain that we would add on and would not have to worry about another payment on top of our already tight budget. So we waited on the Lord, not quite knowing how He was going to do this.

For Mother's Day that year, my husband had carved five wooden mushrooms out of cedar (as yard ornaments), very much like some I had seen and oooed and ahhhed over in Wisconsin on a trip to my Gramma's house for Easter. I was so thrilled; he had put a lot of love and time into them. Spring was in the air, everyone was out gardening, and my mushrooms were getting quite a bit of attention. People were stopping and knocking on my door, inquiring where I had gotten them.

After about a week of that, we decided to make a few and put them in our yard for sale. They ranged between a foot and three feet tall, but we sold them all for five dollars each, no matter what size they were. When we made our very first sale, I jokingly said as I put our first twenty-dollar bill in a special box that sat on top of our refrigerator, "Here is our first savings toward our addition." We all laughed at the time but later realized that was exactly what it was. God's provision added up a little at a time in our little box, at five dollars apiece, and turned into four thousand dollars. (That's a lot of mushrooms!)

In September that year, our fifth child arrived, another boy, Nathan. We remained snug in our little house until July of the next year. That's when we reached our goal of seven thousand dollars. All mushroom money. Our whole family had pitched in; even the youngest had a part in the production of our endeavor. Now it was time to add on.

The end result was that we had enough money, almost right down to the last dollar. Doing the work ourselves and with help from friends and family, we finished the project without borrowing any money.

Not only did our house grow in size, but our faith grew as well. We saw firsthand that when you trust our Lord, He provides in His way and His time. A situation that seemed way too big for us really was too big. But it wasn't too big for our God. Looking back, I see that God took what seemed to be impossible and solved it with something as silly as a carved wooden mushroom.

We have lived in our home for forty-eight years, and God has blessed our family as it has grown even bigger with the marriages of all five children: Lisa and her husband, Mark, parents of Lexy, Grace, and Caleb; Joe and his wife, Ashley, parents of Bailey, Ella, and Vivian; Nick and his wife, Nikki, parents of Colton, Cayden, and Cali; Tony and his wife, Lizzie; Nathan and his wife, Sadie, parents of Drake and Reid.

Once the grandchildren started coming along, we added on one more time. We have been so grateful to have all five of our children with our wonderful daughters-in-law and a great son-in-law living within seven miles of us.

I

Instead, speaking the truth in love, we will
grow to become in every respect the mature
body of Him who is the head, that is, Christ.
—Ephesians 4:15 (NIV)

THERE IS NO ONE PURER of heart than a child. They naturally speak honestly. Sometimes their honesty is actually a little hard to take.

It was my fifty-seventh birthday, and we had our children and grandchildren over for our typical meal and cake celebration. Being that my birthday is in January, we were all saying that it was hard to believe another year had gone by so fast!

Our granddaughter Ella, who was five years old at the time, asked, "Gramma, how old are you?" But before I could answer her, she went on to say, "You must be at least twenty-five, because you have some of that crumply skin starting." Eeeek!

It was a compliment and a blow all in one quick moment. Oh, how we love their honesty.

William Shakespeare said, "No legacy is so rich as honesty." Not everyone understands how vital honesty is. Honesty and trust go hand in hand. When you know someone to always be honest, then they normally gain your trust.

The book of Proverbs repeatedly talks about integrity. The definition of integrity is: the quality of being honest and having strong moral principles; moral uprightness. I might add "even when no one else can see or hear me." A good question to ask ourselves is: am I the same person in public as I am in the privacy of my own home?

It makes me wonder how many times I could have saved someone embarrassment if only I had been honest. That dress just doesn't flatter you as much as others I have seen on you, or you have a little something on your chin. Or, tougher yet, confronting someone when they are clearly in the wrong, telling the truth in love. Proverbs 24 confirms the importance of honesty, even when it might be painful to hear. When done in love, verse 26 says, "An honest answer is like a warm hug" (Message).

Colossians 3:16 tells us that we are to admonish one another with all wisdom, but the sad thing is dishonesty comes so much easier sometimes, especially when telling the truth is costly or makes us feel uncomfortable. But I think the hardest thing of all is being honest with ourselves.

If we are not honest about our own weaknesses and our sins, we will never see the importance of repentance, and without repentance, we will never receive grace or the free gift of salvation.

The gift that is free to us was very costly to our Lord Jesus. He took on our sins and the full punishment for those sins. The truth is if we really want a relationship with our heavenly Father, honesty is imperative. He will accept nothing less.

Second Corinthians 8:21 says, "For we aim for what is honorable not only in the Lord's sight but also in the sight of man" (ESVN).

We all know in our hearts that what is written in Proverbs10:9 is right on, because it says, "Whoever walks in integrity walks securely, but whoever takes crooked paths will be found out" (NIV). He knows!

Heavenly Father, You know me. You know the crooked paths I have taken; You know the times I have fallen into believing the lies the enemy has whispered. I am so grateful that You pick me up and brush me off. You remind me that I am a child of the King and send me on my way with the promise that You are walking by my side. I know I am not alone. Amen.

2

In peace I will lie down and sleep, for You alone,
Lord, make me dwell in safety.
—Psalm 4:8 (NIV)

MY DAUGHTER, LISA, HER HUSBAND, Mark, and their
two girls, six-year-old Lexy and four-year-old Grace Elizabeth,
were on a family vacation. It had been a long day of traveling,

and Mom and Dad were exhausted. The girls were still wound up from all the excitement of the day. They all climbed into bed in the hotel room. Every time things seemed to quiet down, Grace would tell them she wasn't tired, and she'd chatter on about something that happened during the day.

They continued to tell her it was time for her to settle down, but she said she just couldn't sleep. Out of desperation, Dad told her to close her eyes and count sheep.

Finally, the room was quiet. Everyone else started to dose off, until a soft, sleepy voice broke the silence. "Done. I have nine sheep, and two piggies, and a cow."

There is a cute saying: when you can't sleep, don't count sheep; talk to the Shepherd. How many nights has sleep been lost because our minds just will not shut down and rest? We are either rehashing our yesterday or planning out our tomorrow.

Scripture is so clear on how to help those sleepless nights. Proverbs 3:5–6 says, "Trust in the Lord with all your heart and lean not on your own understanding; in all your ways submit to Him and He will make your paths straight" (NIV).

OK, there is the problem. Sometimes we have a hard time submitting to Him. We want to run our own lives. We have our own ideas of how our lives should go. The question that we have to ask ourselves is, do we really trust Him in all areas of our lives?

Think about it. He has a perfect plan for us, but God's plan for us requires surrender and total trust in Him. When we do that, we will sleep like a baby.

Lord God, thank You for the many nights that started out sleepless, and then You calmed my heart and settled my wandering mind, which was running from one thought to another. Trusting in Your complete care and love for me has been a blessing and brings me rest when I am weary. Amen.

3

He said to them, "Go into the world and
preach the gospel to all creation."
—Mark 16:15 (NIV)

IT WAS SUNDAY EVENING. WE were just getting our shoes
and jackets on to head out the door for Sunday-night prayer service,
and we were running a little late. Our six-year-old grandson,
Colton, had spent the afternoon visiting and playing games with
Grandpa and Gramma, and the day had gone by so quickly.

As we were walking out the door, the phone rang, and my
husband suggested we let the call go to the answering machine. So
I grabbed my cell phone, thinking I would call whoever it was on
my ride to church. But as the machine turned on, an unfamiliar
voice came on saying, "Mother's surgery went well. She's in
recovery. I'm waiting for a call back from her doctor to give you
more details." I grabbed my house phone to get the number off
the caller ID so I could call this woman back to let her know she
had dialed the wrong number. I knew that it was important to get
that message to her family. They would be waiting.

As I climbed into the car, I explained to the others what the call was, and I was going to call her back. My grandson didn't miss a beat as he said, "Gramma, just tell her you knew she had the wrong number because your mom was doing fine, and she is in heaven, probably playing checkers with Jesus right now."

Even at his young age, Colton knew that his great-gramma had put her trust and life in God's hands. And she was now with Him for eternity.

How many people do we know who have never gotten the most important message, the one about Jesus? His is a life-changing message of unconditional, unfailing, never-ending love. Do they know we can trust Jesus to save us from punishment for our sins, and we can have eternal life with Him?

Take the time to pass on that message of hope. In the world we now live in—with Twitter, texting, email, and Facebook—we have so many opportunities to spread the message of good news every day. With some people, we won't get a second chance!

I ran into a classmate I hadn't seen in fifteen or so years. He was in line in front of me at a grocery store. We had gone to school together from second grade through graduation. We lived in the same small town, yet I had not run into him for years. We chatted about life and how quickly time passes. Where did those years go? We talked about our family and the weather. But I didn't talk about the most important thing in my life, the Lord.

Two days later, I got the news that he had passed away very unexpectedly. My heart ached. I didn't know whether he knew the Lord or not, but I agonized over the fact that the Lord had given me a chance to share my faith with him, and I did not.

In 1 Peter 3:15, the Bible says, "But in your hearts revere Christ as Lord. Always be prepared to give an answer to everyone who asks you to give the reason for the hope that you have. But do this with gentleness and respect" (NIV).

The greatest way we can show we care about another person is by sharing the gospel of Jesus with them. Live your life in such a way that you will have no regrets.

Oh my heavenly Father, forgive me for failing to share my faith in You with others. For the many times when I heard Your call, but I just refused to step out in faith because I was afraid to fail, or I just didn't have enough faith in You working through me. Help me to share my story of redemption to all that I encounter. Amen.

4

You will keep in perfect peace those whose
minds are steadfast, because they trust in You.
—Isaiah 26:3 (NIV)

THREE-YEAR-OLD DRAKE AND I SPENT a lot of time
together. Most week days from eight until three, it was just the
two of us until we went to pick up his cousins at school. Then we
had a gang for him to play with.

On this particular day, there was a flu bug going around that
his cousin, Cali, was struggling with. So before bedtime, he and
his mom and dad prayed for her to feel better.

As soon as he got to my house the next morning, he ran in the
door and immediately asked if Cali was feeling better. I told him
yes, she was. She had even gone to school that day. He grabbed my
hand and pulled me into the front room where we always pray. He
said very matter-of-factly, "Well, that's because Mom, Dad, and I
prayed for her last night." Then he said, "Oh, Gramma, will you
pray for me so that I feel better? I have the flu bug now."

He already knew, at three years old, that when he was in trouble and needed help with anything, he would turn to the Lord. Why do we insist on trying to do everything on our own, when all we have to do is ask the Master for help?

God is able, in every situation in life, to give us wisdom, strength, protection, guidance, healing, grace, forgiveness, courage, faith, and the list goes on and on.

God actually desires for us to be dependent on Him. Philippians 4:6–7 says, "Do not be anxious about anything, instead pray about everything. Tell God what you need, and thank Him for all He has done, and the peace of God, which surpasses all understanding, will guard your heart and your mind in Christ Jesus" (NIV). What a great promise.

Then in Psalm 50:15, the Bible says, "Trust in Me in your times of trouble; I will rescue you, and you will give Me glory" (NLT). These are such beautiful passages in scripture and great reminders of His faithfulness.

The Lord truly is glorified when we put our trust in Him for our care, like Drake did. What an amazing God we serve!

Lord Jesus, so many times You have pulled me out of the woes of life and reminded me that You were there. Sometimes I am my worst enemy. I want control. You are always faithful to remind me that I can trust in You, to let go and give You back the reins. Thank you, Father. Amen.

5

For we are God's handiwork,
Created in Christ Jesus to do His good works,
which God prepared in advance for us to do.
—Ephesians 2:10 (NIV)

IT WAS LATE FALL AND a beautiful day. We were enjoying unusually warm weather for the beginning of November. We decided to take advantage of these last nice days before winter to spend some time outside. Oh, how I love being outside to smell the fragrance of fall leaves in the great Upper Peninsula of Michigan. There is no place like it.

Vivian and Cayden were both three at the time, and they were having a great time riding the three-wheel bikes around and around in my driveway. They were squealing and laughing. There were many calls to me, "Gramma, watch this! Watch me!" I was telling them their older brother and sister had spent many hours having fun on those same bikes—just like they were. Vivian rode her bike over, stopped in front of me, and asked in her sweetly innocent and cute little voice, "Gramma, when you were a little gramma, did you ride this bike too?"

I know the Bible says that in heaven we will all receive new names. But for now, I never get tired of hearing the name Gramma. It's music to my ears.

I know beyond a shadow of a doubt that He created me to do exactly what I am doing—caring for the little ones. In John 15:16, Jesus says, "You did not choose me, but I chose you and appointed you, so that you might go and bear fruit that will last and so that whatever you ask in My name the Father will give you" (NIV).

I know whatever our job is, or wherever God has placed us in life, we can bear fruit for the Lord by sharing the loving message of the Lord with all those around us. As the song goes, "They will know we are Christians by our love."[1]

When I was eighteen and graduating from high school, I received a scholarship to attend an art school in Chicago. The thought of going off to a big city alone had no appeal to me at all. My heart's desire was to marry my high school sweetheart and have lots of children.

That is exactly what I did. I became a stay-at-home mom, which was not a popular thing to do. I was lonely because most everyone I knew was a working mom. I was blessed to have a sister-in-law, Kris, who lived nearby and, like me, was a stay-at-home mom with my niece and nephew. She was there for me, and I thank the Lord for her. Financially, it was tough, but the Lord helped us out many times along the way when it seemed it would be impossible for me to stay at home. He always provided in ways that never ceased to amaze us.

Romans 8:28 reminds us of how He takes care of us: "And we know that for those who love God all things work together for good, for those who are called according to His purpose" (ESV).

We were so grateful because it made it possible to do what we felt was best for our family, for me to stay at home and care for our five children. Then He placed our eleven grandchildren in my care.

I realize that all of us influence those around us in one way or another, and we, in turn, are influenced by others. The Lord has a plan and a purpose for each of us, and we need to pray diligently, seeking God's direction for our life.

The world is pulling all of us in a direction where moral standards are a huge contrast to a Godly perspective. I am so blessed to share the things that are the most important in my life with the little ones. First and foremost is the Lord's deep, unconditional love for us and His written word. My faith and love for Him are so important. I am able to share all the ways He has blessed me with these children and help them recognize His love and care for them.

Lord Jesus, thank You for Your abundant care for me. Thank You for directing me and providing in desperate times of need. As always, I ask You to help me to understand Your plan for this day. I am so grateful that You are sovereign over my life. Help me to continue to recognize Your voice and will for my life. Amen.

6

Be joyful in hope, patient in affliction,
faithful in prayer.
—Romans 12:12 (NIV)

REID WAS EIGHTEEN MONTHS OLD. I had cared for him while his mom and dad worked. We loved our time together, and all was going well until a few months ago. He started doing something very strange. He would be playing just fine in the other room until he would look up at me, and then he would start to cry. He would run over by me and want me to pick him up, and he would wiggle his fingers in front of my face. It was very apparent that he was unhappy about something, but I just couldn't figure out what it was. Every time, it was the same. He would look at me, cry and run to me, want to be picked up, and then wiggle his fingers in front of my face. It was so odd.

It was really tough on both of us for a couple of weeks, and I had no idea what was wrong. Most of the time, he seemed very content and happy. But there were those strange moments.

During this time of frustration for both of us, I started to connect the dots. I realized that when I picked him up to console him, I would take my glasses off. He would instantly stop crying and become happy. He would get a contented look on his face, climb down from my arms, and go back to playing.

I only use my glasses for reading. For several days, I didn't wear them at all, and he was back to being a very happy boy. We had no problems at all.

I decided to test my theory. While he was playing with one of his favorite toys, I talked to him. He was smiling and happy. Then I slipped my glasses on, and sure enough, that was it. He came running in, and when I picked him up, immediately his fingers were wiggling in front of my face. I took the glasses off, and he stopped and was happy.

Strangely enough, my son Nathan and his wife, Sadie, and his Granny Jannie all wear glasses, and he has no problem with any of them at all. I'm the only one. This continued for several months, and I had to hide my glasses and sneak them on. I tried to reason with him, but as everyone knows, at that age they don't always grasp what we are trying to tell them.

I can think of times in my life when I was discontented. I was unhappy about certain situations. I wanted things to be different. Like Reid, I would make life miserable for those around me because I didn't like the way things were. Did it ever help the situation to have a bad attitude? No, not even one time that can I think of.

Proverbs 14:30 tells us, "A heart at peace gives life to the body, but envy rots the bones" (NIV). That seems pretty harsh, but if we think about it, when we are unhappy about something that we can't change or control, we physically feel rotten. We can think our way into feeling pretty hopeless.

On the other hand, when we are content and not allowing ourselves to wallow in self-pity or envy the life someone else has, we can walk through any situation with a joyful heart.

We have a choice: stay bitter or get better. I believe we have to start by going into the presence of the Lord, thanking Him for any and all the blessings that we do have. When we make the choice to get better, even when our hearts seem so troubled, we can find amazing joy in the midst of our present hard situation. It has happened to me over and over.

Worshiping our God who deserves all glory and honor will give our hearts a peace beyond understanding, even before the situation changes.

James 1:2–4 says, "Consider it pure joy, my brothers and sisters, whenever you face trials of any kinds, because you know that the testing of your faith produces perseverance. Let perseverance finish its work so that you may be mature and complete, not lacking anything" (NIV).

There it is—a golden nugget. We will lack nothing we truly need. Walking through a storm hand and hand with the Lord causes us to grow up, and it completes us.

My Lord God, how grateful I am that You will not allow me to remain in the pit of despair. In all my dark troubled times, You were by my side and brought me through my heartache to see the beauty on the other side. Thank You for the many times that You reminded me of my many blessings. I pray I will never forget. Amen.

7

So that your giving may be in secret. Then your Father,
who sees what you have done in secret, will reward you.
—Matthew 6:4 (NIV)

MY DAUGHTER WAS PLANNING A ladies' retreat out at her
cabin. There was a lot of planning and preparing in the weeks
beforehand, so my grandson Caleb, who was six at the time,
colored some banners to decorate the doors and walls. They were
a hit at the retreat. The ladies were very touched at all of the time
and effort he put into his artwork.

The following Sunday, as their family was getting ready for
church, she told him, "You will probably get some hugs from the
ladies at church today for your nice signs."

He looked so disappointed and said to her, "Hugs? I thought
I would get a dollar."

Oh, how disappointing life can be when we have high
expectations for something. We do a good deed for someone,
and then that sinking feeling comes when they don't seem to
appreciate it as much as we thought they would.

At that point, we need to look at our motives and ask ourselves that tough question: did I really do the good deed for the benefit of someone else or to gain some approval or a reward for myself instead of the Lord? In Matthew 5:16, the Bible tells us to "let your light shine before others, so they may see your good deeds and glorify your Father in heaven" (NIV).

Oh, how easily we slide down that slippery path of seeking self-gratification for things in this world. We may start out with good intentions, but sometimes we want to know, what's in this for me? It might just be acknowledgment. After all, look what I did. Look how much time I put into that. Shouldn't I get something out of this?

Colossians 3:23–24 encourages us by saying, "Whatever you do, work at it with all your heart, as working for the Lord, not for human masters, since you know that you will receive an inheritance from the Lord as a reward. It is the Lord Christ you are serving" (NIV). By doing things unto the Lord, we will never be disappointed. We know someday our reward will be in heaven.

We may never see the fruit of our labor here on earth. But the Bible is clear in 1 Corinthians 2, when it tells us no eye has seen, and no ear has heard, and no mind can conceive the things God has prepared for those who love and serve Him. We can only imagine. It truly is exciting to think about. When we work and our labor is unto the Lord, we have a lot to look forward to.

Oh Lord, thank You for a healthy body, that I can work daily and fulfill Your mission You have planned for me each day. I long to see Your glory in heaven, but I am grateful for the chance to serve You here on earth. Amen.

8

Cast all your anxiety on Him
because He cares for you.
—1 Peter 5:7 (NIV)

CAYDEN HAD JUST TURNED FOUR but was still very attached to his "blankie," as he called it. When he was tired or if he had been hurt, he would immediately look for it for comfort.

We were at the cabin one Saturday, and most of our family was there. The grandchildren were busy playing outside. It had rained the day before, so the ground was wet. The men were busy digging a ditch for a new power line, so there was a lot of mud everywhere.

I could see Cayden was getting tired, and he asked me if he could have his blankie. I told him it was too wet and muddy outside. I explained that it would get all dirty, and then he wouldn't be able to sleep with it tonight when he got home.

A few minutes passed, and again he came to me, asking if he could go into the truck. I just couldn't say no, so I opened the door for him and lifted him in. He grabbed his blankie, and like he always did, he spun the blanket between his thumb and fingers, checking out each corner until he found the favorite one that was worn out from love.

He sat there rubbing it for about thirty seconds with a very contented look on his face, then threw the blanket back onto the truck seat and said, "I'm okay now."

I think I learned a lot that day from my little grandson Cayden. During our busy days, when we are feeling stressed and tired, we need to take a few minutes and turn where we will find comfort, our Lord. There are so many distractions; we feel the need to talk to a friend or our spouse or mom. But the best place to go is to the feet of our Lord.

It is said that God is never to blind to your tears, never deaf to your prayers, and never silent to your pain. He sees, He hears, and He will answer according to His great wisdom of what is best for us at the time. Psalm 119:76 says, "May Your unfailing love be my comfort, according to Your promise to your servant" (NIV).

Lord, forgive me for all the days that I was too busy and distracted to spend time with You. Help me to remember that there is nothing in this world that is more important than the intimate relationship with You, my heavenly Father. Amen.

9

The plans of the Lord stand firm forever, the
purposes of His heart through all generations.
—Psalm 33:11 (NIV)

WHEN LEXY, OUR OLDEST GRANDDAUGHTER, turned
nine, all she thought about was turning ten. It seemed to be her
favorite subject to talk about. Everyone in the family knew Lexy
couldn't wait for her next birthday. Finally, when the big day
came, she was excited to let everyone know she finally turned, as
she called it, "double digits."

I am amazed when I think back to when I was the age of a
single digit. I, too, couldn't wait to be a teenager. Then I couldn't
wait until my sixteenth birthday and the excitement of getting a
driver's license. Next came graduation, and then I couldn't wait
for that magical moment as I looked forward to my wedding.
Then I couldn't wait until I would have a child. After the baby
was here, I couldn't wait until I would be able to sleep all night
again with no wake-up calls in the middle of the night from a
hungry baby.

There is a saying: be careful what you wish for. Before you know it, they are going off to college. Do we wish our life away, waiting for the next thing? We need to live each day with a purpose, and what better purpose could there be than helping someone understand fully how much the Lord loves them?

In Proverbs 19:21, we are reminded, "Many are the plans in a person's heart, but it is the Lord's purpose that prevails" (NIV). There are people in this world who God has appointed you to reach out to, and they will connect with you like no other. Divine appointments we call them. We need to be prayed up and dwelling in the Word of God enough to fulfill God's appointed plans each time they are put before us.

Psalm 118:24 says, "This is the day that the Lord has made, let us rejoice and be glad in it" (ESV). Grab hold of each day, thanking the Lord for it. Look at each day as a blessing, a gift from God. He alone can bring fulfillment in life.

We need to remember that we came into this world only by the grace of God, and when we leave this life, we will take nothing we have accumulated here on earth with us. The exception to that are those people we helped to see the need for God in their lives. We can make a difference in this world by taking each day the Lord blesses us with and making it count. As the old hymn goes, "Make me a blessing to someone today."

Oh Lord, help me to understand Your plan for today. Please help me focus on the needs of others. Open my eyes to those who are hurting; fill me with Your compassion, that I may be a connection between the lost and my Lord. Show me the purpose for my life. Amen.

10

Come near to God,
and He will come near to you.
—James 4:8 (NIV)

THREE-YEAR-OLD CALI LOVED TO TALK to me on the phone. I just loved her precious voice, and each conversation was a treasure of its own. She told me all that had happened each day, and as she shared her heart, it warmed mine. Most of the time, each call ended with the same question, "Gramma, can I come over for a couple of whiles?"

Now how can you say no to that sweet little question? I loved spending time with her.

The Lord longs for us to visit with Him daily as well. When I begin my mornings in prayer with the Lord, I find there is no better way for me to start my day. Jeremiah tells us in chapter 29, verse 13, "You will seek Me and find Me, when you seek Me with all your heart" (NIV). We need to put our whole heart into our relationship with the Lord. He deserves nothing less. James 4:8 shows us, "Come near to God and He will come near to you"

(NIV). When we set aside that time each morning to spend with the Lord and His Word, it helps us feel His presence all day long.

In John 14:13, scripture says, "And I will do anything you ask in my name, so that the Father may be glorified in the Son" (NIV).

The truth is His love is deeper for us than we will ever comprehend. The same God who created the universe wants a relationship with us.

He also is willing to do anything for us, in order to draw us closer to Him. Isn't it amazing when we really take the time to think about it? We can call on the Lord and spend "a couple of whiles" any time we want.

Lord God, I am so grateful to be able to come to the foot of Your throne any time I wish. Thank You for Your overwhelming, unconditional love. Thank You for another day to serve You. Guide my heart today, that I may fulfill Your perfect plan that You have set before me. Amen.

II

Commit everything you do to the Lord.
Trust Him and He will help you.
—Psalm 37:5 (NLT)

FIVE-YEAR-OLD DRAKE AND I WERE reading the story of Jonah and the big fish one day. This particular story was from the book *Read Aloud Bible Stories* by Ella K. Lindvall. It is one of his favorite Bible stories, and this author does a wonderful job of presenting Bible stories at a level that preschoolers can understand.

This particular story goes as follows: "Jonah was not happy. Jonah said, 'I don't want to go do what God says. I will run away.' Jonah hurried down the road. Jonah got on a boat on the blue water. God saw Jonah go. God knew what Jonah needed."

At that point, Drake spoke up and said, "Gramma, I think Jonah needs a time-out."

Yup, that's just exactly what God did. He put him in a time-out in the belly of a big fish.

I think of the times in my life when I knew exactly what God wanted me to do. I was to forgive and pray for someone, or even talk to someone about the Lord. But, like Jonah, I didn't want to forgive or help them turn to God and understand His plan for them. There were people I was angry with, times that I didn't think I should let go of a hurt or forgive. It was in those times that I, too, would spend my time in a time-out of sorts, while God would help me understand that His will and plans are perfect.

The truth is this: what greater thing is there in the world to see than someone turning their life around and following the Lord? Someone makes bad choices and leaves a path of hurting people along their way, and then the Lord opens their eyes to recognize His deep unconditional love for them. How wonderful to see them repent, turn their life around, and run to God.

They are no different from me, a sinner saved by grace. Sometimes in my Jonah-like judgment of others, I don't see them worthy of God's love or my time. But the Lord does! There is no better end to any story than to see a life changed for Christ.

I need to spend time daily with Him so that I always recognize His voice when He calls me to a task for one of His heavenly appointments.

My Lord God, I know I can't do this without Your help. Only You can change my hardened heart. Help me to forgive as You forgave me. Please give me the compassion, words, and strength to forgive and truly love those who are lost and hurting. Amen.

12

Yet You, Lord, are our Father.
We are the clay, You are the potter,
we are all the work of Your hands.
—Isaiah 64:8 (NIV)

I WAS ON MY WAY to pick up some of my grandchildren from school when I heard an odd sound coming from my car. The grandkids in the car asked me what the noise was.

I didn't know, so I called my daughter at their business in town. She and her husband owned a service center. She told us to come right away and she would have their mechanic look at it.

Well, it ended up taking more time than we thought it would. I decided to call my daughter-in-law, who would be expecting the kids to be home our usual time; I wanted to explain why we would be late. I told her I found out the car problem was nothing detrimental and that we should be on our way soon.

When I got off the phone, my thirteen-year-old grandson, Colton, asked me what detrimental meant. I told him it meant that it wasn't anything dangerous. He asked how to spell it, so I told him. He said, "Great. I am going to use that in my homework because it will make me sound intelligent."

We don't have to pretend to be something or someone we are not. We are all unique, each created for God's purpose. God never makes mistakes, yet so many of us suffer with insecurities. I myself was very quiet and never felt like I fit in, nor did I feel like anyone even noticed I was there. But the Lord noticed me, and He notices you as well. The good news is I don't ever have to look to myself for security, because I find that in Christ alone. Psalm 9:10 says, "Those who know Your name put their trust in You, for You, Oh Lord, have not forsaken those who seek You" (NIV).

He has created each of us with our own personality, our own identity. From the beginning of time as we know it, scripture says God created all men equal. Hebrews 10:10 says, "And by that will, we have been made holy through the sacrifice of the body of Jesus Christ once and for all" (NIV). We are all perfectly made in His likeness.

We, like Colton, are all wonderfully made in His image. So that means our self-worth is the value God placed on us when we were born.

My Lord and God, thank You for helping me find my value in You. You alone are worthy of worship and praise. Amen.

13

The righteous cry out, and the Lord hears,
He delivers them from all their trouble.
—Psalm 34:17 (NIV)

IT WAS A BUSY DAY at my house with six of my grandkids over. There were two seven-year-olds, two four-year-olds, and two who were three. They were so full of energy that day. It was winter and a very cold day, so we were held up inside. They always seemed to find something to do. It amazes me how they think of things like indoor baseball with a pool noodle and a balloon. They were having a great time when all of a sudden I heard crying. I investigated the situation and made peace. A few minutes went by, and then we had another small incident. Cayden, one of the three-year-olds, who had already won himself the spot on my staircase for a time-out sentence to be served, was having a rough day. It was his second time.

The steps are near my kitchen, where I was busy preparing supper. I usually like to sit and talk to each child when they have misbehaved. Doing so gives me a one-on-one chance to discuss what happened, why it was wrong, and what they need to do differently next time. It is especially important when they are three years old, because they need to be encouraged to do the right thing next time.

He and I were having a great conversation, when all of a sudden we heard Ella crying in the playroom. Cayden immediately threw both hands up in the air and exclaimed, "I didn't do something, Gramma!" He was proudly proclaiming his innocence.

Adam and Eve started the whole mess with sin in the Garden of Eden when they chose to do wrong. Their fall from grace started when they disobeyed God by eating the fruit from the forbidden tree.

The serpent had told them that if they ate the fruit, they would be like God, and their eyes would be opened. They would know good from evil. But it didn't work out like they thought it would.

Genesis 3:22–23 tells us this: "And the Lord God said, 'The man has become like one of us (Father, Son and Holy Spirit) knowing good and evil. He must not be allowed reach out his hand and also take from the tree of life and eat and live forever.' So, the Lord God banished them from the Garden" (NIV).

We know that it is stated clearly in the Word of God that when Adam and Eve sinned, it unfortunately opened the door for immorality in the world. But they did gain the sense of right and wrong by eating fruit from the forbidden tree.

We know that we all are born with the ability to discern right from wrong. We were also born with the freedom of choice. Unfortunately, we don't always choose to do what is right. When we do wrong, it exposes our rebellious nature.

There is a nudging in our heart when an unkind thought comes. We need to restrain ourselves from allowing it to go from a thought to words that are spoken, which can never be retrieved and taken back, or an action that once set in motion can never be reversed.

The good news is that God has sent the Holy Spirit to those who choose to serve God. The Spirit helps guide us and convicts our hearts when we make bad decisions. In those moments of our lives, instead of proclaiming our innocence like Cayden did, we need to take responsibility for our actions and admit our guilt.

On the day of Pentecost, Peter spoke the words from Joel 2:29, 32: "I will pour out my Spirit in those days ... and everyone who calls on the name of the Lord will be saved" (NIV). The Bible tells us in Acts 2:37–38 that when he spoke, the people's hearts were turned and they wanted to know what they should do. Peter told them to repent and be baptized in the name of Jesus Christ. By making that choice, we will be saved from the punishment of hell.

He went to the cross for each and every one of us. He knew we would fall over and over. And yet He loved us so much He took on all of our sins. He made it possible for us to share a portion of heaven with Him.

Palms 62:8 says, "Trust in Him at all times, you people; pour out your heart to Him, for God is our refuge" (NIV). We need to trust Him, because we can never do enough good, or be good enough, to get to heaven on our own. He paid it all, the full price of our redemption.

Father in heaven, I am so grateful for the gift of salvation and the pouring out of the Holy Spirit. So many times in my life, You overwhelmed me with Your presence, comforting, guiding, revealing truths, and interceding on my behalf. I am amazed by You. Amen.

14

My heart says of You, "Seek His face!"
Your face, Lord, I will seek.
—Psalm 27:8 (NIV)

I WAS SO HAPPY WHEN my son's family started attending church again. His three little girls were getting a little easier to take on the outing to church: Vivian was two; Ella was three; and Bailey was six. They just loved Sunday school and children's church.

The following Saturday night, the three girls had a sleepover at my house. They were going to come to church again with Grandpa and me, and we would meet Dad there. Breakfast was a buzz of excitement and chatter; they couldn't wait to go back again. It brought back memories of the days of getting my own five little ones ready for church. Those were very busy days, and I think we always ended up being late or at best walking in at the last minute. But today, Ella was all dressed, ready, and standing by the door, waiting for her sisters. She turned to me and said very excitedly, "I sure hope they talk about Jesus again today!"

Those words warmed my heart, but at the same time, they made me question: am I that excited to hear about Jesus? Do I long for him as I did when I first came to know Him as Lord and Savior of my life and began my walk with Him? Am I overwhelmed by His holiness? Do I long to honor His commands like it talks about in Psalm 119? Do I hunger for His Word and His will in my life like I long for things of this world?

We live in a world where people long for all sorts of things: new cars, a nicer home, a better job, a different significant other, a long weekend, more money. Once obtained, all of these things eventually just don't satisfy.

Cars rust away, and there is always something new that catches our eyes. The weekends are never long enough. We see things that don't satisfy within the new house, and we want to remodel. We find flaws in our spouse or boyfriend or girlfriend that we want to correct. And most of us never feel we have enough money to make ends meet because, let's face it, we keep stretching the ends of our budget by adding one more payment or loan for something we really didn't need anyway.

When we long for a deeper relationship with the Lord, which is obtainable, it doesn't cost us a penny. It does mean we need to take more time for Him, but the payback is immeasurable, and that relationship is always precious and always remains fulfilling.

Someone once told me that when being baptized, he had asked the pastor to hold him under the water for a minute. He truly wanted to see if he longed for a relationship with the Lord as much as he longed for his next breath.

The beautiful thing is He longs for us. The Lord of all creation longs to have a relationship with us. Isaiah 30:18 tells us, "The Lord longs to be gracious to you ... He rises up to show you compassion" (NIV). I need to let that sink in, because at times I let this broken world around me swallow me up. I ask myself, what are the things of this world that I long for daily?

It wasn't long after Jesus was in the desert, where He fasted for forty days and nights, that He said, "Blessed are those who hunger and thirst for righteousness, for they will be filled" (Matthew 5:6 NIV). Jesus was giving the Sermon on the Mount when He spoke those words. Hunger and thirst were still fresh in His memory. He had not eaten anything during those days in the desert, even when Satan tempted Him. But He fed on scripture and used it as a weapon when His enemy attacked Him.

It was a good reminder to me. The importance of John 6:35 comes to mind, when Jesus said to them, "I am the bread of life; whoever comes to Me will not hunger, and whoever believes in Me will never be thirsty" (NIV).

Someday we all will stand before Him. I do long for that day!

Lord God, help me to recognize anything that I am putting before You. Help me to hunger for You and only You, as Ella did. Lamentations 3 tells us Your steadfast love is new every morning. Help me to see it with fresh, new perspective each day. Amen.

15

Then Peter came to Jesus and asked,
"Lord, how many times shall I forgive my
brother or sister who sins against me?
Up to seven times?" Jesus answered, "I tell you
not seven times, but seventy-seven times."
—Matthew 18:21–22 (NIV)

BAILEY AND COLTON WERE BORN six weeks apart.
About the time they were three years old and at Gramma's while

their moms worked, it was very busy. They loved to play together, and they were inseparable. They played so well most of the time, but they did have their moments. On this particular day, they seemed to have a lot more moments than usual. I was constantly refereeing the disputes.

At one point, I had finally had enough of their bickering. I sat down with the two of them, looked each one in the eye, and told them if there were any more incidents, they would each have a time-out. They both sheepishly nodded.

Only a couple of minutes later, I heard the two of them battling again. I headed to the front room to see what was going on, just in time to see Bailey pinch Colton on the arm. Folding her arms across her chest, she stated, "Bailey time-out" and headed for the staircase where the time-outs were always served.

I hadn't been there to see what Colton had done to make Bailey so upset, but evidently it was something that made her angry enough to feel the punishment was worth it.

First Peter 3:9 says we need to try something completely the opposite. It reads "Do not repay evil for evil or insult for insult. On the contrary, repay evil with blessing, because to this you were called so that you may inherit a blessing" (NIV).

Then the question I have would be this: is revenge ever worth it? Revenge is like a snowball rolling down a hill covered with heavy wet snow. It starts out small, like a thought of retaliation. The more we allow it to roll around in our minds, the bigger it gets. In both cases, the bigger they get, the heavier they are, and the harder they are to deal with. Then the snowball effect reaches out to everyone around us, whether we want it to or not. It only makes our hearts bitter and cold, and it changes who we are. Revenge never mends our broken hearts; it tears us apart inside.

The only way to stop the pain of a wrong done against us is to forgive. Only true forgiveness can mend a heart that is damaged. When we forgive, it breaks the stronghold that anger and hatred have on us and relieves the pain of the painful moment that has taken control of our lives. Most of the time, that pain causes sleepless nights and steels the joy from our days. Forgiveness restores; then healing can come to not only you but also to the one who hurt you.

We need to remember the words in the prayer Jesus shared with His disciples as He taught them how to pray. It is recorded in both Matthew 6 and Luke 11. He tells us we need to forgive those who have sinned against us just like He has forgiven us. Sometimes the hurt and pain are so deep, daily forgiveness is required. But when we recognize our own brokenness and sin and the fact that we have been washed clean, it helps us let go and let God take over. He mends our broken hearts and gives us the strength to forgive.

I believe the most important thing that occurs when we forgive is the breaking down of the sin wall of anger, hatred, and revenge that has built up between us and God because of the unforgiveness. Forgiveness always restores the relationship to the one who loved you enough to die for you, the Lord Jesus Christ.

Holy Spirit, help me recognize my own sinfulness before I judge others. Lord, please give me the strength to not only forgive but to pour out grace and mercy, as You do on me, in those times when there is a need for restoration. Amen.

16

If anyone has material possessions and sees a
brother or sister in need but has no pity on them,
how can the love of God be in that person?
—1 John 3:17 (NIV)

FOUR-YEAR-OLD DRAKE AND HIS DAD were planning an ice fishing trip with his uncles and a friend of the family. Drake's best friend was supposed to be coming with his dad as well. He was pretty excited about spending the day with his friend Jase.

It was the end of March, and they were trying to get the last fishing trip in before the ice became unsafe. They figured there might be some slush on the ice, so Drake's dad told his friend to be sure to bring rubber boots. In the phone conversation, my son found out that Jase had outgrown his boots from last year and might not be able to come because of the situation. But Nathan told him that would not be a problem because Drake had just gotten a new pair; his old ones would still fit him, and he offered to let Jase use Drake's brand-new boots.

Now, these new boots just happened to be blue, Drake's favorite color. And they just happened to have dinosaurs on them, which happened to be Drake's favorite thing. As you can well imagine, when Drake overheard his dad's phone conversation, he was really struggling with this plan. After all, he was excited about wearing those new boots himself. He had told all of his cousins and Gramma about them.

When his dad got off the phone, Drake told him that even though Jase was his best friend, he didn't think he should have to share his new boots with him. Nathan decided this was a good learning moment for Drake. He began to explain that if Jase had two pairs of boots and Drake had none, he was sure that Jase would let him use them.

But Drake was still not sure it was a good idea. So his dad told him that Jase would not be able to come because he had no boots, and he told him it would be very selfish for him not to share.

It led to a great discussion of what selfishness is and how it hurts God's heart, and how we have to fight against selfishness. He said that Jase would probably be hurt also. Drake thought about it for a while and was pretty quiet. They were on their way home in the truck, so Nathan gave him time to think about it. When he finally glanced into the back seat, he could see Drake gritting his teeth, his forehead all wrinkled, with every muscle in his little body tensed up. Very puzzled, Nathan asked him what he was doing. He said, "Dad, I am fighting selfish."

Wow, that is a tough battle for all of us. Hebrews 13:16 tells us, "And do not forget to do good and share with others, for with such sacrifices, God is pleased" (NIV). I believe we have all struggled with selfishness in one form or another, from babies all the way up to old folks. Selfishness seems to creep into our lives so quietly and unassumingly. The scary thing is that while we really don't recognize it in ourselves, it seems so easily detected in others. When you think about it, selfishness is one of the greatest sins because it seems to be at the root of many other sins.

It is a very tough spiritual battle, but maybe Drake has the right idea. If we stop, grit our teeth, and think things through before we make some decisions, maybe we can fight selfish too.

My Lord, please open my eyes to my self-centered thoughts and actions. Help me see the needs of others and act on it. Please remove the blinders that I want to keep on so that I can remain in my own selfish world. Help me to share out of compassion and love for others and my deep love for you. Amen.

17

For it is with your heart that you believe
and are justified, and it is with your mouth
that you profess your faith and are saved.
—Romans 10:10 (NIV)

I HAD A BEAUTIFUL MOMENT with my grandson Cayden one day. We were sitting on the floor face-to-face. He was six years old, which is one of my favorite ages. At six, they love to sit and have conversations. He had grown to be so thoughtful and tenderhearted. He asked why we couldn't see Jesus and asked where Jesus was.

I carefully explained that Jesus was everywhere, and we could talk to Him anytime we wanted. Then I told him how much Jesus loves him and wants to be our best friend. I told him if we ask Jesus to be our friend and our Lord, He will live in our hearts forever.

He was very quiet for a minute; I could see he was seriously thinking about what I had told him. Suddenly, a broad smile broke out on his face, and he exclaimed, very excitedly, "Gramma, I can feel Jesus in my heart right now!"

We did not realize that his three-year-old sister, Cali, was standing behind me, taking in everything that we were saying. She dropped down to her knees next to her brother, with her hands on her neck and teary eyes. She said, "Gramma, I can feel Jesus in my throat!" We all hugged. What a blessing to see Jesus right there.

No matter what we have done, God has made a way for us to be set free. Jesus gave His life so that we could not only have eternal life but live a life filled with moments of unexpected glory, beginning at our spiritual birth. That moment in our lives when we recognize that we can never be good enough on our own to get to heaven is that time when we recognize our deep need for a Savior.

Even at a young age like Cali and Cayden, we can honestly look at our lives and see how much we need a Savior. We feel the emptiness that needs to be filled with something more than earthly things.

It is so important to make time each morning, when the new day is fresh, to be alone with the Lord, asking for His help and wisdom for each person and situation we will encounter each day. Take the time to let His love overwhelm us, like it does the little children. We need to make the choice of living a fulfilling life unto Christ. It is then that we will feel Him in our hearts, and sometimes, like Cali, we can even feel Him in our throats.

Oh Lord, You amaze me daily when You give me exactly what I need each day. Your supply is endless, and You know better than I do what will draw me closer to You. Thank You for the right words at just the right moment. Thank You for Your endless unconditional love. Amen.

18

If anyone thinks they are something,
when they are nothing, they deceive themselves.
—Galatians 6:3 (NIV)

ONE WEEKEND IN THE FALL, our whole family was at my daughter and son-in-law's cabin having a work bee. It was a cloudy gray day, so the kids were inside playing a board game on one of the beds. They were having a great time. There was a lot of squealing and laughing.

As I was stood watching them, all of a sudden, the sun broke through the clouds and was shining right in eight-year-old Colton's eyes. He asked if I would pull the shade for him. I did what he asked, and then I took the opportunity to explain to them that someday when we get to heaven, there will be no sun or moon. It was one of the stories in the Bible that had always fascinated me, so I was happy to share it with the kids.

In Revelation 21:23, we are told, "The city does not need the sun or the moon to shine on it, for the Glory of God gives it light, and the Lamb is its lamp" (NIV).

Colton looked at me and said, "Gramma, you must be really close to heaven." I was pleased that he thought so. I thought he was speaking of my sharing the verse in the Bible, until he added, "You must be, what, at least fifty-five years old already, aren't you?" It sure took the wind out of my sails.

Pride is a sin because we are living a self-centered life instead of living our lives centered on Christ. A few verses come to my mind: James 4:6 says, "God opposes the proud but shows favor to the humble" (NIV). Proverbs 11:2 says, "When pride comes, then comes disgrace, but with humility comes wisdom" (NIV). We selfishly want to take credit for something that is not even ours.

Jesus is the greatest example of humility. Mark 10:45 tells us, "For even the Son of Man did not come to be served, but to serve, and to give His life as a ransom for many" (NIV).

There are more than one hundred verses in the Bible that talk about being humble. Humility is not weakness. It is actually the opposite. It is only when we recognize the need to turn to God for His strength to fight the battle against pride that we can, for the moment, have victory.

Pride and selfishness go hand and hand, and there are consequences to being prideful. We cannot live in fellowship with God when we don't recognize God's sovereignty over our weakness.

In reality, can we ever really take credit for anything? Isn't all the knowledge we have only ours by the grace of God, the one who gives it to us?

Oh my Lord, You oh Lord are my Savior and King. I come before You, Lord, recognizing how dependent I am on You. Please remove the pride that remains in me and replace it with humility. Open my eyes to see where I do not have complete dependence on You, so that I can live fully in Your will and grace. I pray in Your precious Son's name, Jesus. Amen.

19

Do not be overcome by evil,
but overcome evil with good.
—Romans 12:21 (NIV)

OUR DAUGHTER, LISA, SON-IN-LAW, MARK, and their four-year-old son, Caleb, had gone out to dinner one night to their favorite place. When they walked into the restaurant, it was empty except for a man and woman sitting at a table. As they were walking by that table to get to their seats, it was evident the couple was having a disagreement. The three of them smiled and said hello, to which the husband returned their greeting, but the wife remained silent and sullen. Well, just as they got right next to the couple's table, my grandson paused and said, "Mom, she's looking at us with angry eyebrows."

We all know that sometimes the timing of a child's honesty is just not good. To say the least, my daughter and son-in-law were mortified. They could think of nothing to say.

The poor woman got caught. I wonder how many times the expressions on my face give way to what is really in my heart.

Truth hurts at times, and yet once we see ourselves clearly as we truly are, through the eyes of others, and more importantly the eyes of our Lord, it helps us recognize how desperately we need God in our lives. To think my heart has not ever been where hers was would be a lie.

The good news is that He loves us too much to leave us that way. Psalm 139:23–24 says, "Search me, God, and know my heart, test me and know my anxious thoughts. See if there be any offensive way in me, and lead me in the way everlasting" (NIV). When we recognize our need and ask the Lord to show us those areas in our lives that have to be changed, He is faithful to respond.

That process sometimes is very long and painful. At times, it is only through our suffering that we seek Him for help and growth in our walk with Him.

If we are willing to respond with a humble heart when He reveals the ugliness of our sin nature and confess our sins, followed by seeking His wisdom in the Word of God, He has this promise for us in Philippians 1:6: "And I am sure of this, that He who began a good work in you will bring it to completion at the day of Jesus Christ" (ESV).

The completion comes when our life on earth is done and we reach our final destination. We will never be perfect on this side of heaven. In the meantime, I strive daily to submit my will so that I can live out His will. The Bible says He will make our path straight. God is in the business of transforming hearts and lives. We all have hope, and we know He is faithful to restore and redeem.

Lord, I turn to You when my heart is not in a place of joy or contentment. When I know my outlook on life is not with a grateful heart, only You can give me peace in my times of trouble so that I can face the world. I pray that all will recognize that my hope is in You, my Lord. Amen.

20

Be very careful, then, how you live—
not as unwise but as wise, making the most of
every opportunity, because the days are evil. Therefore do
not be foolish, but understand what the Lord's will is.
—Ephesians 5:15–17 (NIV)

WHEN OUR GRANDSON DRAKE WAS three, he loved fruit snacks. He would do just about anything to get some. One morning when he and his mom, Sadie, were on their way to my house to drop him off before she went to work, he had a snack attack and asked Mom if he could have some fruit snacks. Mom told him no, it was way too early to have them.

He was very persistent and begged her, but the answer remained the same. He was quiet for a little while, so Mom checked on him in the rearview mirror just in time to see him with one hand raised in the air. His eyes were closed, and she heard him say, "Jesus, I was going to have fruit snacks for breakfast and share them with you, but Mom said no."

Oh my goodness. I guess that could be considered double manipulation. He was testing God and Mom at the same time. I am so glad we serve a God that cannot be manipulated but a God who can be trusted. His plan is undoubtedly always what is ultimately best for us.

Sometimes we are like Drake. Things seem to sound or look so good at the moment, but they may not be good for us at that time. The problem is, once the seed of deceit is planted, it is hard to turn back. We want what we want! Then at times we act like a three-year-old, thinking we know what is best for us, and we have a hard time taking no for an answer.

There have been times in my life when I wanted something so badly it would consume me. I felt it was something I needed. I prayed relentlessly. At the time, I couldn't understand why God would not answer this prayer. It seemed so right. At times, discouragement and fear would set in, and it was then that I would try to take control.

My form of manipulation was a little different from a three-year-old's. At times, we try to bargain with God, making promises to change something in our lives or do something for someone in need. We all know that God cannot be convinced to do anything that is not in our best interest.

We know God has a perfect plan. Jeremiah 29:11 says, "For I know the plans I have for you, declares the Lord, plans to prosper you and not to harm you, plans to give you hope and a future" (NIV). So we pray, we trust, and we wait.

Oh Father, You intimately call me Your child, and Your hand is always guiding me in the right direction. But way too often, I veer off of the path You have made for me. Like Drake, I become self-focused and stubborn at times. Please help me to trust and obey. In Your precious name I pray, Jesus. Amen.

21

And we know that in all things God works for the good of
those who love Him, who have been called according
to His purpose.
—Romans 8:28 (NIV)

I HAVE A HAMMOCK IN my backyard on which all of my
children and grandchildren have had hours and hours of fun. One
of their favorite things to do is for all the kids to climb on and
have me tell the story of Noah's ark or Jonah. I rock them gently
while telling the beginning of the stories. But when the time
comes for the storms in the stories, I swing the hammock wildly
back and forth, and they all scream with delight.

This particular day, it was just Vivian and Cali, seven and
four respectively. Right in the middle of Jonah's stormy boat
ride, Vivian asked me to stop. She said that she had something
important to ask me. She looked so serious. She said, "Gramma,
when you and Grandpa die, could all of us cousins live at your
house? We all love it here."

I told her nothing would make Grandpa and me happier, and I hugged her. Then she added, "We figured Bailey and Colton are twelve now, so they are old enough to take care of us." *So*, in the eyes of a seven-year-old child, Grandpa and I, at the ages of sixty-one and sixty-two, were not long for this world.

I was blessed, first of all, to grow up across the street from my grandparents. Then I was further blessed to live in Gramma and Grandpa Tomasoski's house and raise all of my children there. Now I get to share lots of memories here with my grandchildren. My gramma was only fifty-two when she passed away. I was only eight years old, so I cling to the memories that I have of her and my grandpa.

Oh, how fast the years have flown by in my lifetime. We certainly don't know what our future holds, but we do know who holds our future, and He knows the end of the story.

Proverbs19:21 says, "Many are the plans in the mind of a man, but it is the purpose of the Lord that will stand" (ESV). I guess when I think about it, my plans usually are self-focused and worldly. They are things that will not matter when I am gone from this world. He has an eternal purpose for me each day that I spend here on this side of heaven. So I ask to understand what His will and plans are daily and for His help to fulfill them.

I can take comfort in knowing that my life rests in the hands of the one who has redeemed me for His own.

Oh Lord, thank You for the blessings of children and the view of life through their eyes. They fill life with wonder. We never know what they will say next. Like Vivian, I want to look to the future with great expectations. Thank You, Lord. Amen.

22

Finally, all of you, be like-minded, be sympathetic,
love one another, be compassionate and humble.
—1 Peter 3:8 (NIV)

IT WAS THE CHRISTMAS SEASON, and we were all at church on a Sunday morning. We were singing one of my favorite Christmas songs, "What Child Is This."[2] My five-year-old granddaughter, Ella, was sitting next to me. I glanced down at her in time to see that she was singing with her whole heart, and the tears were rolling down her rosy little cheeks. When the song was over, she looked up at me with big tears in her eyes and said, "Gramma, that song made my eyes water."

When we see things through the eyes of a child, we understand Jesus's command in Matthew 18:3 when He says that we must become like little children to enter the kingdom of heaven. They are so honest, sincere, open, and trusting. They display their love and compassion openly without embarrassment or shame. As we get older, we want to hide our emotions. Why is that?

There is a story in scripture that gives a clear example for us to follow. In John 11:32–38, we are told that Jesus saw Mary weeping because her brother had died. He showed compassion and even wept with her. This story of Jesus miraculously bringing Lazarus back to life after being dead for three days was always a mystery to me. He knew his friend was going to come back to life, yet He wept with Mary and Martha, Lazarus's sisters. He showed such deep emotion. There is a lesson in that.

When you look up the word *compassion*, you see that it originated from the Latin word *compati*, which means "to suffer with." More than forty times, the word *compassion* is mentioned in the Bible. Many times it is describing the attributes of God our Father and Jesus our Savior. This means that God suffers with us when we are in the midst of a fiery trial. That overwhelms me with tears, just like Ella, when I take the time to reflect on it.

Second Corinthians 1:3–4 says, "Praise be to the God and Father of our Lord Jesus Christ, the Father of compassion and the God of comfort, who comforts us in all troubles, so that we can comfort those in any trouble with the comfort we ourselves receive from God" (NIV). It is calling us to allow someone else's heartbreaking situation to become our heartache as well.

If we are truly compassionate, it will change the way we live. We will rejoice with those who rejoice, and we will hurt with those who are hurting. It would cause us to think more of others and less of ourselves and then act on it.

How different the world would be if we all answered God's call in Colossians 3:12: "Therefore, as God's chosen people, holy and dearly loved, cloth yourself with compassion, kindness, humility, gentleness and patience" (NIV).

Oh my Lord, please open my eyes to those around me who need an encouraging word. Help me to hurt with those who are hurting. Fill my heart full of compassion so that I can show love and kindness. Lord, please give me the words to encourage them to seek You and Your Word in their times of trouble and pain. Amen.

23

The righteous cry out, and the Lord hears them;
He delivers them from all their troubles.
The Lord is close to the brokenhearted
and saves those who are crushed in spirit.
—Psalm 34:17–18 (NIV)

I HAD A VERY BUSY house on this particular day. Eight of the youngest grandkids were there. My house is very noisy and hectic on these days. If there is a phone call, it is usually very short, or I do callbacks after the troops are gone.

Unfortunately, I had to make an important call that day. After making sure the kids knew how quiet they must all be, I dialed the phone. Things went pretty well while I was on hold, but as soon as I got to talk to a real person, two-year-old Cali fell off of the toy she was sitting on and bumped her head pretty hard.

I asked the woman to hold on and explained my dilemma; she said no problem. I tried to console Cali, hugging, kissing, talking to her, but nothing seemed to calm her or stop her crying. She did have quite a good size bump on her poor little head.

Then the cookie jar caught my eye, so I thought I would take a stab at giving her a chocolate chip cookie. OK, I was desperate. I held it up and said, "Here, maybe this cookie will make your head feel better."

She had such a pathetic look on her face, but she did stop crying and put her hand out to take it from me. Immediately, she put the cookie right on the bump in the middle of her forehead and said with such sad eyes, "Yes, that made it feel better."

In our times of pain and hurt, we sometimes look to things for a quick fix to ease our heartache. But the things of this world hold no promise to properly mend our troubled hearts. Sometimes our choices actually make things a lot worse. God's Word reveals truths that lead us on the path to finding the calm during the storm and draw us on a closer walk with Him.

No matter what the issue is, turning to the Lord for help is the only way to hold steady through a tough time. Whether problems are big or small, short or long, He is our rock to cling to.

In Psalm 18:1–2, David is being hunted down by King Saul. His life is in grave danger. It is here that he shows us where to turn in times of trouble. "I love you, the Lord, my strength. The Lord is my rock, my fortress and my deliverer, my God is my Rock, in whom I take refuge, my shield and the horn of my salvation, my stronghold" (NIV).

We know without a doubt that we can find comfort in the Lord no matter how big the bump in the road is. God is the answer. So, curl up in your favorite chair with God's Word and a chocolate chip cookie. I know without a doubt that your heart will feel better.

My Lord, how grateful I am to be able call on You each and every time I feel inadequate to deal with something in my life that is troubling me. You are so quick to answer with wisdom and guidance from Your Word. I feel your presence, and it calms my heart. Amen.

24

You will be enriched in every way so that you can
be generous on every occasion, and through us
your generosity will result in thanksgiving to God.
—2 Corinthians 9:11 (NIV)

LEXY IS OUR OLDEST GRANDDAUGHTER, and she has a
heart of generosity. She always makes sure friends and family have
their share. When she was eleven, her gramma Pat encouraged

Lexy and her sister, Grace, to take piano lessons. Their time slot was right after school.

The routine was to stop at McDonald's (our only fast-food place in town) and grab something to go to keep their stomach from grumbling for the hour. Every time, Lexy had the same request: she wanted to know if she could get something for her piano teacher. Mrs. Fish was such a good sport, and the three of them would have a little picnic together before the lessons began. Lexy would beam from ear to ear.

We think of the great command that is recorded in Mark 12:30–31: "Love the Lord your God with all your heart and with all your soul and with all your mind and with all your strength. The second is this: Love your neighbor as yourself. There is no commandment greater than these" (NIV). That is what Lexy was doing, loving her neighbor.

When we take the time to send a card or text to someone just to let them know we are thinking of them and that they are important to us, we are loving our neighbor. We can be a listening ear and support someone going through a tough time or serve them in a time of need. At times, it means giving up a want of our own to buy something that is needed by another. Taking that action is loving our neighbor as ourselves.

In 1 Corinthians 1:24, we are told, "No one should seek their own good, but the good of others" (NIV). Then Galatians 5:14 says, "For the entire law is fulfilled in keeping this one command: Love your neighbor as yourself."

These are not suggestions; they are commands!

Unfortunately, those commands in scripture are contrary to the world we live in today. Selfishness reigns everywhere we look, whether on Facebook, television or radio ads, magazines, newspapers, and in the millions of books available to us. They all tell us how to find our happiness by doing things for ourselves. They push you to find *your* joy, do what makes *you* happy. The world wants us to gratify our selfishness.

God shows us the secret to true happiness, and it begins when we follow these commands and truly love everyone around us. When we put that into practice every day, it is life changing. If everyone focused on the needs of others, like Lexy did, just think how that could change the world. In truth, when we do something to make someone else happy, it automatically brings us joy and true happiness.

Oh Father, thank You for the wisdom written in Your Word, and thank You for the conviction from the Holy Spirit in the many times I seek self-gratification instead of looking at the needs of others. Help me follow these commands. Amen.

25

Therefore, I tell you, whatever you ask for in prayer,
believe that you have received it, and it will be yours.
—Mark 11:24 (NIV)

I HAVE A WONDERFUL SON-IN-LAW. A few years ago, I
mentioned how I would love to have a bigger garden in my yard,
but we have so many trees we don't have an area that has full sun.
He immediately asked, "How big do you want it? We have a lot
of room here in our yard." After I told him the size, he smiled
and said, "I'll take care of it."

He sure knows how to win a mother-in-law's heart! Early
that spring, I had a big, beautiful garden all fenced and ready for
planting. He even brought in many dump truck loads of very
fertile soil. It was more than I ever expected.

We got to work and began the process. All of my grandkids
help with planting, weeding, even hauling sand in the toy dump
trucks from the sandbox to the garden for my rows of carrots.
Their help makes gardening a joy, and they have a great feeling
of accomplishment when the vegetables start to grow.

At six years of age, Caleb was with me one day when I went to the garden to pick beans. I was so frustrated when I found all of my plants had a mold growing up the stems, and the leaves were all shriveling up. It had happened so quickly, and they were starting to rot.

In my many years of gardening, I had never experienced anything like this. I was so disappointed because more than two-thirds of the plants were wilted, brown, and covered with the mold. My hopes of having a good crop of beans to share with family and friends were squashed.

Thinking out loud, I said, "Well, maybe I should have prayed before we planted." I had trusted in my own abilities and wisdom and had not looked to the Lord for His help with the garden. My dad taught me how to garden when I was growing up because I helped him in the garden. I also trusted in my forty years of gardening experience to grow a good garden, but I had not once asked the Lord for His help.

I told Caleb he would need to remind me next spring to pray before we plant. Caleb said, "Gramma, why don't we pray right now for them?" I didn't want to discourage him, but I knew it was too late. There was no way those plants were coming back to life. But I didn't want to squelch his enthusiasm to pray in all things. So we prayed and thanked God for what was growing well, and I went home very discouraged.

About a week later, we went back to the garden, and as we approached the fence, Caleb let out a squeal of joy. "Gramma, the prayers worked! God made the plants grow back!"

Sure enough, the dead stems were still standing, and now there was a clump of green leaves and the beginning of blossoms right at the base of each stem. I was speechless. I couldn't believe my eyes. I had never seen anything like it. Only God could have brought those dead plants back to life.

In Matthew 11:25, scripture talks about having the faith of a child. It was very clear to Caleb where those green leaves had come from. He didn't have to understand the mystery or miracle. It was enough to know God loved him and answered his prayers.

So often, we want to analyze the situation, and then we miss the blessing that God intended for us. Psalm 9:9–10 reminds us: "The Lord is a refuge for the oppressed, a stronghold in times of trouble. Those who know Your name put their trust in You, for You, Lord, have never forsaken those who seek You" (NIV).

So we need to do like Caleb did. Seek Him in prayer and then trust in His loving care for what is best for us.

Lord, You are mighty and so faithful to come to my aid in times of need. You hear my cries for help, and You in Your wisdom answer me. Life here on earth is hard and uncertain, but I know without doubt I can always count on You. You know my heart. I am so thankful to You, Father. Amen.

26

Before they call, I will answer; while
they are yet speaking, I will hear.
—Isaiah 65:24 (NIV)

AT THIRTEEN, GRACE HAD HER last game of basketball
for the season. It was what they call a nail biter. From halftime
on, it was a one- to two-point spread, and each team took turns
taking the lead. But now we were behind by two points, and it did
not look good for our team. Just seconds before the final buzzer
was to go off, the opponent had the ball, and when they took a
shot, they missed.

Grace got the ball on the rebound. She started to head down
the court but realized she was out of time. She stopped and threw
the ball for what seemed to be a very slim to no chance shot. We
all held our breath but really felt she didn't stand a chance at that
distance. You can imagine our excitement when the ball dropped
right in the basket for a very long three-point shot.

We had won the game and the tournament. The team ran
to Grace, surrounding her, and they all hugged. The crowd

had jumped to their feet and were clapping and cheering with excitement. I asked Grace later how it felt to make the winning score. She said, "I couldn't believe it. I just chucked the ball, and I was as surprised as everyone else that it went in."

When we see the desire of our heart before us, we need to take that chance, like Grace did. Pray first, and then walk by faith, not by sight.

Psalm 37:4 reminds us of this: "Delight yourself in the Lord and He will give you the desires of your heart" (NIV). First, we need to ask ourselves, does my want line up with scripture? Is this God's will and His best for me? Will this desire draw me closer to the Lord or pull me further away? Matthew 7:7 tells us to "Ask and it will be given to you; seek and you will find; knock and the door will be opened to you" (NIV).

So even when it seems to be a long shot, we need to place everything at the foot of the cross and let the Lord have control. If we see doors opening, that means He is providing a path. Then we need to be obedient and move forward. If the doors close, we know it is not His will or plan for our lives. It's a win-win way of doing things. He always has the final say, and we know it's His best for us.

My Lord, I thank You for the many times You answered yes to my prayer when I had a deep desire for something I felt I needed. But I also praise and thank You for the many things to which You answered no. Looking back, I am so grateful for Your wisdom and intervention in situations. I realize now that when You said no, it would not have been a good thing in my life at that time. Praise your name, Jesus. Amen.

27

Beloved, let us love one another, for love is from God,
and whoever loves has been born of God and knows God.
—1 John 4:7 (ESV)

WHEN VIVIAN WAS FIVE, SHE and I were rocking one day in my big chair. I had read her a few books, and we were just talking. I hugged her and told her I loved her. She smiled and said, "I love you too, Gramma, but I love Jesus more than anyone in the whole world." Aww, that's the way it is supposed to be. It was music to my ears.

To me, the saddest thing in life is seeing a lost soul, someone who refuses to recognize God for who He is. Whether we choose to believe in Him or not, He believes in us; He loves us even when we refuse to accept Him. Lost souls completely depend on themselves, and the pressures of this life are crushing and lonely.

One thing lost people seem to have in common is a never-ending desire to fill the emptiness they feel with things of this world that will never satisfy. There is always a feeling of wanting more: Now, if I could only get a_____, or if I could only take the vacation I have dreamed of, then I will be content. Or if I can find that perfect person, a soul mate, it will fill that emptiness.

Nope. Nothing of this world will do it. Sure, there are things that make us happy for a while, and we have loved ones we are grateful for. But let's admit it: every shiny, new thing loses its luster, and every person lets us down one way or another. Then it's on to the next thing or the next somebody.

What a lot of people don't understand is the fact that the emptiness, that void, is something only God can fill. God, and God alone, can bring peace and joy to our hearts, even in the lowest moments in our life.

In the book of Luke, a young man asks Jesus, "What must I do to inherit eternal life?" In Luke 10:27, Jesus answers him, "Love the Lord your God with your heart and with all your soul and with all your strength and with all your mind and love your neighbor as yourself" (NIV).

When we admit we need Jesus and cannot live life without Him, when we accept that He is Lord and bend our knees to His will, we realize we need to totally surrender our lives. Then His love pours over us, like nothing in this world will ever do, and it is never changing and never ending. The safest and most peaceful place on earth is in the center of God's will. His love fills that huge void we have, and it is only then that we realize He is all we ever really need.

Lord, like Vivian, I am overwhelmed by Your love. I feel so unworthy, and yet I know my worth comes only from knowing and surrendering my life to You. Praise your holy name. Amen.

28

My dear brothers and sisters, take note of this:
Everyone should be quick to listen, slow to speak,
and slow to become angry.
—James 1:19 (NIV)

MY SON-IN-LAW MARK SAW AN opportunity one winter. When the snow was piling up, he made backyard luge for the kids and Gramma. He spent a lot of time piling up the snow with his skid steer at a place at the end of the driveway where there is a long, natural hill. It was great fun. This particular day, I had brought three-year-old Cayden to play with his cousin Caleb, who was then four years old.

We had spent about an hour and a half on the hill, and they were having a lot of fun making many runs. But they were getting tired from walking up the long hill. Cayden decided he wanted to rest and play on the swings down in the yard for a while. Caleb thought it sounded like a good idea and followed behind his younger cousin. Cayden reached the swing set just as it dawned on Caleb that there was only one good swing out of the two, and he was not going to get it.

All of a sudden, Caleb let out a big sigh and flopped on his back in the snow. I knew he was upset. As I walked by, I asked him if he was going to join us by the swings. He said, "No, Gramma. I am talking to God."

I knew my daughter had been helping him understand that when he got angry, he should take a minute or two with God and ask for help to control the anger so that he wouldn't say angry words that would hurt someone's feelings.

I was pretty sure that was what he was doing. I smiled and thought of how pleased and proud of him I was. He was only four, and he was already seeking God's help in times like this. After a few minutes, he came and joined us, and I asked if he had had a good talk with God. He said, "Yes, Gramma. I asked God if He would help my cousin Cayden learn how to share better!" Hmmm.

That sure made me think of the many times that I have done the exact same thing Caleb did. I would go to the Lord with a problem that involved someone else and ask the Lord to change that person's heart, instead of taking responsibility for my own actions and asking where I needed a heart change.

When we truly take the time to examine our shortcomings, or, let me say it plain and simple, our sin, when we go before the Creator of the universe asking for wisdom in a situation that is difficult, scripture tells us what to do. The Bible tells us in James 1:5–8, "If any of you lacks wisdom, you should ask God who gives generously to all without finding fault, and it will be given to you. But when you ask, you must believe and not doubt, because the one who doubts is like a wave of the sea blown and tossed by the wind. That person should not expect to receive anything from the Lord" (NIV).

James wanted us to know how to not only get through difficult trials but to joyfully get through these trials. The only requirement is that we believe. That's it, nothing else. Just *believe*

He will give you the wisdom you ask for to help make right decisions.

I was so blessed when I studied the book of James and found that verse. It truly changed my life! The good news is we don't have to go through those difficult things on our own.

My heavenly Father, so many times I have come before You ready to condemn someone else for something when the truth is I need to examine my own heart. I am way too quick to judge others. Please forgive me, Lord. I am so careless with my thoughts. Amen.

29

The Lord looks down from heaven upon the
children of men, to see if there are any
who understand, who seek after God.
—Psalm 14:2 (KJV)

ONE DAY WHEN DRAKE WAS four, he and his dad were
on their way to my house early in the morning. Drake was being
pretty quiet, which is not normal for him, so my son, Nathan,
looked in the rearview mirror to check on him. He noticed he
was sitting with his eyes closed and his hand on his heart.

He asked Drake what he was doing. Drake's answer was, "I am
concentrating. Do you know what concentrating means, Dad?"

"Yes, I do, Drake. What are you concentrating so hard about?"
his dad asked.

"Well, I am trying to figure out what God wants me to do
today," he said. Now there is a lesson to learn. I wonder how
many days would have gone a lot better if I only would have
asked the Lord what His plan for me was instead of going out on
my own.

Jeremiah 29:11–13 says, "For I know the plans I have for you, declares the Lord, plans to prosper you and not to harm you, plans to give you hope and a future. Then you will call on Me and come and pray to Me, and I will listen to you. You seek Me and find Me when you seek Me with all your heart" (NIV).

What an amazing promise! When seeking God in the morning, He guarantees us that He is listening to us, but when we ask for Him to guide our day, we need to be open to His will. We also have to be able recognize His voice when He calls on us.

The great news is that when we feel God's nudge calling us to do something out of our comfort zone, we don't have to do it on our own. He gives us the strength we will need to fulfill the mission before us by sending the Holy Spirit.

John 14:26 says, "But the Helper, the Holy Spirit, whom the Father will send in my name, He will teach you all things and bring to your remembrance all that I have said to you" (ESV).

I often wonder how many divine appointments I have missed out of fear of failure, or for the lack of humbling myself to recognize I never had the ability on my own anyway. I know it is imperative to just trust the Lord to take control, and then I can work though the task before me and get it done.

Heavenly Father, thank You for Drake's reminder to seek Your will each day. I am grateful that You guide and protect me. Help me to surrender my will in order to fulfill Your perfect plan for each day. Lord, I do hunger to know Your will. Amen.

30

So whether you eat or drink or whatever you do,
do it all for the glory of God.
—1 Corinthians 10:31 (NIV)

COLTON LOVES GOING TO THE cabin with Grandpa to bait the deer for deer season. He helps fill the bucket with corn, sugar beets, and a head of cabbage. One day, I had made a big pot of soup for everyone at the cabin and called the kids to the table for lunch. Colton took one look at the cabbage in his bowl and stated, "Gramma, why did you waste good deer food?"

I guess it's all in our perspective or our point of view. Adrian Rogers says, "Wisdom is looking at life from God's point of view." The Bible is filled with life-changing wisdom. Taking just a few minutes a day to gain new insight from the Word of God is truly life changing. I can't even begin to think how much better my life would be if in each decision I make, I would take the time to think of what God's point of view is instead of my own.

Lord, I thank You for Your many blessings in life, one of which is to see my large family at our cabin, working and playing together. As I look around, I see how differently You have made each of us. Yet we are all Your children, created in Your image. Thank You for the gift of family. Amen.

31

Above all, love each other deeply,
because love covers over a multitude of sins.
Offer hospitality to one another without grumbling.
—1 Peter 4:8–9 (NIV)

WHEN SIX-YEAR-OLD ELLA WAS IN first grade, I drove five of my grandchildren to school every morning. Our routine was to begin the trip by praying for them and their families. I would always ask them if there was anyone else who needed prayer, and every day, Ella would respond with the same request: "Can we pray for a boy in my class that is mean to everyone and always gets into trouble?"

One day after praying, she asked me why I thought some kids were so mean. I was not sure how to answer that question, but I did tell her that we live in a busy world, and sometimes people don't have the time to show others that they are loved. When they don't feel loved, they just don't know how to treat others with kindness.

Weeks went by, and one day a woman approached me at the school while I was waiting for the kids to come out at the end of their day. She said that my granddaughter had a crush on her son. Ella had sent him a note, simply saying, "I love you." My heart sank as I realized my sweet little Ella had her first crush but had made a bad choice because this was the mom of the little boy we prayed for daily.

I tried to be lighthearted when I teased her later about the crush she had on him. But as I talked, she had such a puzzled look on her face. Then suddenly she said, "Oh no, Gramma, don't you remember? You told me that he might not know that anyone loves him, and that's why he is so mean, so I wanted him to know that someone does love him." Wow, that was true Godly love at its best.

Ella had followed these simple steps. She first turned to the Lord in prayer. Then, when she didn't know what to do, she sought wisdom. Finally, she showed the boy the total unconditional love of Jesus. Scripture says in Ephesians 4:2, "Be completely humble and gentle; be patient, bearing with one another in love" (NIV).

Ella loved unconditionally on purpose. It is easy to love those who are lovable. In chapter 6 of Luke's Gospel, he tells us to "love our enemies and do good to them" (KJV). That kind of love is rare and beautiful. What a great example. It truly humbled me to see such a beautiful witness of Christ's love in this six-year-old. Luke goes on to say that when you love like that, your rewards will be great and you will be children of the Most High, because He is kind to the ungrateful and the wicked. Luke continues by telling us to be merciful, just as your Father is merciful.

It made me look at those around me whom I might find difficult to deal with in a whole new light. Have I ever questioned the difficulties in their lives that had wounded them in a way they haven't been able to overcome? Maybe a heartache that is still ongoing? I know I need to see them through the eyes of the Lord and love as He loves, unconditionally, as Ella did.

Oh Lord, You remind us countless times in scripture that we are to love as You love us. Yet sometimes my heart fails to do what is right. I know I can't do this in my own strength, so I cry out to You to give me a heart filled with loving compassion, forgiveness, and acceptance. Help me, that I may see others though Your eyes and be an instrument of Your love. Amen.

32

My command is this:
Love each other as I have loved you.
—John 15:12 (NIV)

WHEN MY GRANDSON CAYDEN WAS three, he was a very active, busy boy, and like most little ones, he tended to say what was on his mind.

He and his brother, Colton, had a sleepover at our house, and I was taking them home. As we got to their house, Colton hugged me, then ran into the house to tell his mom about his adventures at Gramma and Grandpa's.

When I hugged Cayden goodbye and kissed him on the cheek, he stopped and looked me in the eyes and said, "Gramma, I love your kisses." My heart melted right there on the porch. Oh, how words like that warm our hearts.

How often do we have people in our lives who are such a blessing, and we never tell them how much they mean to us? Words spoken in love are healing and bring joy to others. Why do we hesitate to tell them?

If it is hard to look that someone in the eye like Cayden did, there are many other ways to show you care. Write a note or a card, or even send a text. Spend time with them. Make sure everyone in your life knows you value them and how they are a blessing to you. Kind words spoken can be life changing to someone.

First Thessalonians 5:11 says, "Therefore encourage one another and build each other up, just as in fact you are doing" (NIV).

Please don't let another moment go by. Life is so uncertain. There is no promise that we will have a "next time I see them" moment. Never put off till tomorrow what you can do today. Reach out to those you care about and let them know today.

Lord God, thank You for my family and all the loved ones You have put in my life. Please give me the words to let them know how much they mean to me. You amaze me daily with the blessings You pour onto me through others. Help me bless others in the same way. Amen.

33

As for God, His way is perfect:
The Lord's word is flawless;
He shields all who take refuge in Him.
—Psalm 18:30 (NIV)

WHEN DRAKE WAS FIVE YEARS old, he really enjoyed being a big brother to Reid, who was eighteen months. While we were eating lunch one day, I was having a hard time getting Reid to eat, so I decided to try what mothers and grandmothers have done for years. I remembered my mom using this method to get my younger brothers to eat, and I also fed all of my kids and grandkids like this. I raised the spoon full of food in the air and said, "Here comes the airplane!" Then I made the noise of the engine, hoping the result would be him opening his mouth as the spoon full of food got close.

It worked very well. As he finished the last bite, Drake asked, "Gramma, can you feed me like that? The way you used to when I was little?" It made me smile. Then I filled up his spoon, and the airplane sailed it his way. After the second bite, he looked at me lovingly and said, "Just like old times, hey, Gram."

A good memory warms our hearts for sure. No matter what is happening in our lives today, no one can take away a happy memory. We hold fast to them. Concentrating on memories can bring us through tough times and make us thankful for what we have been blessed with in our lives.

I discovered another way to use memories as a blessing: memorize scripture. I was not a good student in my growing-up years. I really hated school. I would much rather be playing some sport outside. But like everyone else, I had to go through my years of learning. I struggled very much with memorizing. Through my years of reading the Bible, I felt that memorization was something I couldn't do, so I just never tried.

But after participating in a women's Bible study that encouraged memorizing verses, I began to pray for God's help with it. I decided to give it a try. I walk most days for thirty to forty-five minutes, so I wrote out the first five verses of the first chapter in the book of James and recited them while I walked. After a couple of weeks, I could recite the first chapter by memory. I was so surprised and grateful. The Lord walked with me through the book of James. What a life-changing experience it was. I am certain, without a doubt, that if I can do it, anyone can.

When we have God's Word ready in our minds and an unexpected situation comes up, we can be quick to answer the adversary. Jesus was quick to stop the enemy's attacks when He was fasting in the desert for forty days before He started His ministry. He used scripture alone to defeat Satan. When we memorize scripture, we, too, have a powerful weapon against the accuser.

The Word of God is described in Hebrews 4:12 like this: "For the word of God is alive and active. Sharper than any double-edged sword, it penetrates even to dividing soul and spirit, joints and marrow; it judges the thoughts and attitude of the heart" (NIV).

This sword is more powerful than any weapon man has ever made. All we have to do is take the time to know it. It helps us make better decisions. Psalm 119:11 says, "I have hidden Your word in my heart that I might not sin against You" (NIV).

So, if you are apprehensive and feel you just can't do it, ask the Lord to help you. Then put your trust in the one who can help.

Oh Father, I surely understand my weaknesses, and I thank You for being my strength. When I am empty, You fill me. When I am lonely, I feel your presence. When I am weary, You build me up. You know my every need, and You fulfill it. You shower me with blessings. Praise your name, Lord. Amen.

34

I will instruct you and teach you in the way you
should go; I will council you with my loving eye on you.
—Psalm 32:8 (NIV)

ONE NIGHT WHEN CALEB WAS three, he was saying his
nighttime prayers with my daughter, Lisa, kneeling by the side of
his bed. He had his head bowed, eyes closed, and hands folded. He
was going through his list of each family member that he would
ask the Lord to bless when Mildred, his very large, eight-month-
old Lab and Mastiff mix puppy, ran into him and knocked him
down.

Without missing a beat, he got back up into his praying
position and asked, "God, why did you make Mildred so big?"

His mom leaned over to him and said, "Caleb, God made
dogs all different sizes."

He turned, looked at his Mom, and whispered to her, "I
wasn't talking to you."

Caleb did the right thing: He sought the Lord's wisdom
instead of his mom's or dad's. It seems like when we are in trouble,

we automatically pick up our phone to call someone. Yes, that does seem to lighten our burden, but we need to first turn to the one who truly can help. Psalm 121:2, 8 says, "My help comes from the Lord, the maker of heaven and earth ... the Lord will watch over your coming and going both now and forevermore" (NIV).

Why would we seek wisdom anywhere else? When struggles come our way, we need to talk to God. We must spend time in prayer and in the Word of God. He has the answer to every question.

Oh my Father, I am so grateful to be able to call on You whenever I am in need. Your unconditional love and care for me are overwhelming at times. I know I am never alone; You are my constant companion. Amen.

35

She will give birth to a son, and you are to give
Him the name Jesus, because He will save
His people from their sins.
—Matthew 1:21 (NIV)

MY SON NATHAN AND HIS wife, Sadie, have been very active in praying with the boys each night before bed and before meals. They realized that even when Reid was only fifteen months old, he recognized the name of Jesus.

They went to visit my daughter, Lisa, and her family at their cabin. They found them getting ready to decorate their place to host the Christmas Eve dinner.

Lisa had just pulled out all the Christmas decorations. Seeing the baby, she decided to dig through the many boxes to find a child's nativity set for him to play with.

When they placed the nativity set in front of Reid, the first thing he picked up was the donkey. They took the opportunity to teach him the names of each figure as he picked it up. When he picked up the baby in the manger, they said, "And that is

Jesus." He got so excited he dropped the figure of the baby, and both hands went in the air to praise the name of Jesus. What an example that is for all of us.

We all know that, without a doubt, there is power in the name of Jesus. Philippians 2:9–11 reminds us: "Therefore God exalted Him to the highest place and gave Him the name that is above every name, that at the name of Jesus every knee should bow, in heaven and on earth and under the earth, and every tongue acknowledge that Jesus Christ is Lord, to the glory of God the Father" (NIV).

Only the name of Jesus has the power of salvation. It has life-changing power. He lived here on earth for thirty-two years; and He lived a holy and spotless life, never sinning even though He was tempted. But then He suffered the death of a sinner by His sacrifice on the cross, so that when we trust in Jesus, we can be saved from the eternal punishment that we all deserve.

Acts 4:12 states this: "Salvation is found in no one else, for there is no other name under heaven given to mankind by which we must be saved" (NIV).

In fact, the meaning of the name Jesus is "Savior." The name Christ means "anointed," and anointed is the Greek word for the Hebrew "Messiah." More than five hundred times, you can find Jesus called the Messiah in the New Testament.

I can tell you that the spoken name of Jesus warms my heart and calms my fears, brings peace when it doesn't seem possible, fills me with joy, and overwhelms me with the thought of His unconditional love. I, like baby Reid, at times can't help throwing my hands in the air, praising Him for who He is in my life, my Lord and Savior.

My Jesus, I praise Your holy name. Thank You for opening my eyes to see You as You are, Lord of all. Thank You for Your sacrificial love-act of dying on the cross for my sins. Glory to You, Lord. Amen.

36

He heals the brokenhearted
and binds up their wounds.
—Psalm 147:3 (NIV)

IT WAS TIME FOR THE county fair, and all the grandkids
were excited to go. They chattered all day at my house, hoping to
see one another there and ride the different rides together. They
talked about cotton candy, slushes, and the ring toss.

But Ella, four at the time, talked all day about the bounce
house. She didn't care about anything else.

The kids ate quickly. The time had come to go, and off they
went. There was so much excitement and so many things to do.
They would run into friends and family and stop to visit.

When they finally got to the bounce house, Ella went
immediately to the ride, took off her shoes, and ran over by the
door. The young man who was working told her that the kids
who were in there had a few minutes left, so she would have to
wait. As she sat there, more kids came and lined up behind her.

When the time finally came, my son Joe and daughter-in-law Ashley watched as one by one, their little Ella stepped aside and ushered the kids in before her. She was as excited for all the other kids to go in as she was herself. But when she was about to step up inside, the young man put his hand up and said they were at the full limit and she would have to wait her turn.

She was crushed, to say the least. Undoubtedly, the young man had not realized what she had done or seen how she had let the others go first. She was too little to understand, so she made a beeline for her daddy's arms that were stretched out waiting to comfort her. As the tears ran down her cheeks, he hugged her and told her how happy she made him when she had helped all the other kids and let them go before her. You could see her broken heart mending as he gently talked. Then she picked her head off of his shoulder, smiled, and said, "Daddy, you made my heart feel a lot better."

I am so grateful I have a Father in heaven whom I can run to for comfort when I have a broken heart. Our heavenly Father doesn't always fix our problem or change the situation, but He is there to love and guide us to do the right thing. He knows exactly what I need to mend my broken heart, just like Joe did that day with Ella.

There are well over a hundred verses that talk about our loving Father being present in our lives to heal and help us through troubled times. Psalm 34:18 tells us, "The Lord is close to the brokenhearted and saves those who are crushed in spirit" (NIV). Then Psalm 55:22 reminds us to "Cast your cares on the Lord and He will sustain you; He will never let the righteous be shaken" (NIV).

The word *sustain* means strengthen or support, physically or mentally. When we are hurting and walking through something tough in our lives, so often it affects our health as well. We have access through the Word of God to draw close to the one who can comfort us like no other. There truly is a peace beyond all understanding when we walk close to the Lord. We know that whatever our trial is, He knows, He cares, and He will draw us close if we allow Him into an intimate relationship. It's a relationship that cannot be shaken unless we ourselves walk away.

When we choose to stay in His Word and take time with the Father daily, Isaiah 46:4 promises us this: "Even to your old age and grey hairs I am He, I am He who sustains you. I have made you and I will carry you; I will sustain you and I will rescue you" (NIV). Then Psalm 3:3 says, "But you, Lord, are a shield around me, my Glory, the One who lifts my head high" (NIV). Those are amazing promises to hold on to!

My Lord, so many times I have run to You with a heartache, and each time, You walked close to me, breathing life and hope into my emotionally drained spirit. Your Word is a comfort to me at all times. Thank you, Father. Amen.

37

Be merciful, just as your Father is merciful.
—Luke 6:36 (NIV)

IT WAS THE FIRST DAY of school, which is always bittersweet.
We had a very busy summer with kids around me all day, and
now I would only have Drake during the day. It was finally time
to pick the kids up. As five of them got into the car, there was a
buzz of chatter and excitement. Everyone was talking at the same
time. I broke into the conversation, asking how the first day went
and who their new teachers were.

Most years when I've asked that question, I've gotten good
reviews. But this year, one of the kids was pretty quiet and let
everyone talk before they went on to explain that their teacher
did not seem happy, and it was not very good.

Before I could say anything, Bailey, who was twelve, cut into
the conversation. She started to defend the teacher and said, "We
don't know what was going on in her life. Maybe she was stressed
or had a headache or sick or just had a hard day."

I was so proud of her. Not only did she show wisdom in giving the teacher the benefit of the doubt, but she was giving grace and mercy as well.

In Matthew 5, we read the Beatitudes in Jesus' Sermon on the Mount. In verse 7, He said, "Blessed are the merciful for they will be shown mercy" (NIV). There have been way too many times in my life that I judged people way too quickly. It is always much easier to judge than to give mercy. This is especially true in difficult situations when sometimes we feel we have that right to judge and hold our ground. But the truth is God is the only rightful judge. James 2:13 tell us this: "because judgement without mercy will be shown to anyone who has not been merciful. Mercy triumphs over judgment" (NIV).

We have no right to be unmerciful with others when we have been given so much mercy and grace. We really need to realize the full measure of our redemption is due to Christ dying on the cross as the ransom for our sins. He pardoned us fully. When I really let that sink in, it brings me to tears. I don't deserve that. Not one of us deserves that. It's a free gift. Because we have been given that gift, we in turn are to mirror the life of Christ and always, yes always, give grace and mercy. Even when we feel the person doesn't deserve it, we are to obey; it opens the door for the receiver of grace to be overwhelmed, recognizing it can only be Christ through us, and want what we have in our lives: our Savior

There is a great scripture that reminds us of this. Ephesians 4:32 says, "Be kind and compassionate to one another, forgiving each other, just as in Christ God forgave you" (NIV).

God's mercy triumphs over all!

Lord, You are loving, kind, and merciful. You shower us with Your grace. I know I fail far too many times, and yet You forgive and encourage me to do better. Please give me the strength and wisdom I need to give grace and be merciful to all I encounter each day, in every situation. I know I am not capable on my own. Amen.

38

Greater love has no one than this:
to lay down one's life for one's friends.
—John 15:13 (NIV)

CALI WAS FOUR YEARS OLD when her little cousin Drake was born. Every day, she would beg Mom to let her go to Gramma's to see the baby. Oh, how she adored him. I have never seen a little girl love a baby as much as she did. The minute she laid eyes on him, each time she came over, she would say the very same thing: "Isn't he adorable, Gramma?" She would rock him and sing softly to him in her sweet little voice, songs she would make up. The love just flowed from her to that little baby boy.

One day, she came over to spend time with him, but she was acting really oddly. I couldn't figure out what was going on. She was keeping a distance for some reason. She would start to go near him, and then she would back away and just sit and look at him from a distance. She didn't beg to hold him like she did on every other visit.

Finally, she came to me and threw her arms around me, sobbing. She told me that she had a sore throat, and she knew she shouldn't go by the baby. She had been in pure agony, knowing the right thing to do but still wanting to stay near him. She looked up at me with tears, and with her little chin quivering, she asked me to call her mom to come and get her.

I don't think I have ever seen such a great act of selfless love here on earth like I saw that day. She loved him so much that she let go of her wants, for his safety. She was afraid he would get sick like she was. That was true sacrificial love.

God created us all to love and serve Him. That is what the Lord calls us to do daily. To love Him, by putting first and foremost God's will, and then to put everyone else's needs before our own. Truly dying to self.

In Matthew 16:24, Jesus was talking to his disciples and said, "Whoever wants to be my disciple must deny themselves and take up their cross and follow Me" (NIV). Then in chapter 25:40, He told them, "Truly I tell you, whatever you did for one of the least of these brothers and sisters of mine, you did it for Me" (NIV).

It's not always easy to put the needs of others first. It is a daily, conscious effort, with lots of prayer. At times, we start out with good intentions, but it is tough when our wants get in the way.

But the good news is we serve a great God who loves us no matter how many times we fail. He is willing to pick us back up, dust us off, and whisper softly, "Try again. You can do it. I am here to help." We should never give up trying to do what God calls each and every one of us to do.

He is not asking us to do anything He Himself hasn't done. He is the originator of selfless love. He left heaven as a King of Majesty and came to earth as a gentle baby. While on earth, He did not reign as a king, but instead He came to serve and save us all. And He is coming back again! This time, He will come back in power and glory to be Lord over all.

Lord, I know I need Your help to walk through each day and put the needs of others first. Your great example on the cross encourages me. Help me, Lord! I cannot do this alone. Help me daily to battle my selfish thinking. Amen.

39

May Your hand be ready to help me,
for I have chosen Your precepts.
—Psalm 119:173 (NIV)

WHEN REID WAS JUST THIRTEEN months old, he began walking without holding on to anything. He had this walking thing all figured out. As he walked into the front room one day, he spied a rubber horse that is made for little ones like Reid to sit and bounce on. He sized it up. He had seen his brother Drake do this before, so he knew how to put his leg over to straddle it and sit down. He got on after a short struggle, but he leaned too far forward, and both he and the horse fell over. He stood back up, stood the horse up, and struggled to get back on. Once more, he leaned too far forward, and down he went with the same results. He and the horse fell over again. As I watched, he continued to do the same thing a dozen times before I went to rescue.

I think about my life, how many times I leaned on things of this world for comfort or stability, and each time I would have the same result as Reid. I would not be able to stand under the pressure. I have learned to lean on the source that I can trust to hold me up and keep me stable. It is all revealed in the written Word of God. Isaiah 41:10, 13 says, "So do not fear, for I am with you; do not be dismayed, for I am your God. I will strengthen you and help you; I will uphold you with my righteous right hand … For I am the Lord your God who takes hold of your right hand and says to you, do not fear; I will help you" (NIV).

There have been times in my life when heartache was so deep I couldn't think straight, and the Lord held me up. He kept me stable enough to get through each day. He has hand-fed me scripture to nourish me back to spiritual health. I was so broken at one point; I remember just begging Him to help me. On one particular day while praying, I flipped opened my Bible. I was unsure of where to read, but the scripture I laid my eyes on was Psalm 27:14. "Wait for the Lord; be strong and take heart and wait for the Lord" (NIV). My heart was overwhelmed. It made me realize I was trying to control the situation that God and only God could change. That afternoon, I walked into an empty church. It was just me and my Lord. Once more, I poured my heart out to Him. Then I grabbed a Bible there in the pew and just opened it up. When I did, there again, I found my eyes fixed on, you guessed it, Psalm 27:14. Wait for the Lord … It is times like that when we need to heed to the Holy Spirit. So I waited on the Lord. It was a long, steady process, but He healed and restored. Not on my timing but His. I look back and see how in that waiting period, the Lord used that time of a painful trial to help me grow to a deeper relationship with Him.

We always want quick answers and healing, but God in His sovereign plan restores in a way that is not humanly possible. He sees way beyond what we want, and He gives us what we truly need. It is always more amazing than we could ever imagine.

He will not hesitate to come alongside of us when we call on Him. He loves us enough to want what is best for us. Jesus is our pathway to the Father. Jesus Himself tells us in John 14:6, "I am the way, the truth, and the life. No one comes to the Father except through me" (NIV).

Oh my Lord, thank You for the many, many times You have held me up when I was too weak to stand on my own. Thank You for drawing me close and walking with me through trials. Thank You for giving me wisdom to deal with each situation, each time calming my fears, knowing Your will was always the best for me. Praise Your name, Lord. Amen.

40

"In everything I did, I showed you that by this kind of hard work we must help the weak, remembering the words the Lord Jesus Himself said: 'It is more blessed to give than to receive.'"
—Acts 20:35 (NIV)

WHEN COLTON WAS JUST A baby and first began talking, he and I spent a lot of time throwing a little football back and forth. Actually, *football* was his very first word. Oh, how he loved to play catch. He never got bored with it. It seemed like that was all he wanted to do even as he got older.

Well, I had grown up with three brothers and had raised five children, four of which were boys. Needless to say, I had a lot of practice throwing a football.

During one of the birthday parties at Colton's house, all the adults were gathered in the living room visiting. Colton, who was eleven at the time, walked in carrying a football. He looked around the room for a minute and then said, "I was wondering if someone would come out to throw me some passes?" In the room at the time were his dad, two grandpas, and six uncles who had all played football. He then spoke words that warmed my heart: "Gramma, would you mind?"

I know for sure over the years that I had spent many hours tossing a football around, so I could throw a good pass. But I believe it was not because of my abilities that Colton called on me to play ball. It was because I chose to be available.

God blesses us when we pour our time into others. We are commissioned to go out and make disciples of all nations. It starts right in your own home. The best gifts we can give are our time, attention, and love. Philippians 2:4 says, "Let each of you look not only to his own interests, but also to the interests of others" (ESV).

By serving others, we are serving the Lord. Of course, it's pretty easy to say yes to grandchildren. They seem to have a way with us. But there were things I missed out on. Like others who serve in all kinds of different ways, there are many sacrifices we have to make.

I have to be honest. Caring for the children hasn't always been easy. But I wouldn't change a minute of those times. Nothing in this world was as fulfilling as loving those little ones, and, oh, the love I got back. The conversations and the loving hugs were worth their weight in gold.

I cannot even begin to count the bouquets of flowers held in little hands behind their backs. Most of the time, the stems were way too short to put into a vase, so we would have to carefully press them between the pages in my vintage King James family Bible.

I have boxes of artwork that spent their proper time adorning my refrigerator, until the next masterpiece took its place. Every one of those things is a priceless treasure.

Romans 12:10 says, "Be devoted to one another in love. Honor one another above yourselves" (NIV). Oh, what a blessing we receive when we give, because we can never outgive God. The blessings we get back far outweigh what we give.

Father, forgive me for the many times that I have been selfish with my time and the many things You have blessed me with. I know that it is more blessed to give than to receive, and yet I fail so often. Please help me to be aware of the needs of others around me. Amen.

41

Who of you by worrying
can add a single hour to your life?
—Luke 12:25 (NIV)

WE ARE IN THE MIDST of one of the greatest pandemics in many years. Everything is shut down, and family quarantines are in place. Much of our conversation is about this situation.

Even though this is going on, I still am grateful to be able to watch Drake, who is four now, and Reid, who is eighteen months, while their mom and dad continue to work. Their mother, Sadie, is a nurse at our local hospital, so we pray every day for her safety along with the other family members.

One day while Drake and I were eating lunch, the phone rang. It was my daughter, Lisa. We talked for some time, and eventually the conversation turned to what we had heard about the virus. We also were talking about the Spanish flu pandemic that had gone through the country in 1918 and how it came back in the fall that year. People were saying this COVID-19 virus may do the same thing. We talked of the different things that they were using to fight this bug.

I didn't realize that Drake was intently listening to me until I heard him say, "Gramma, Gramma, I know what is going to take that flu away." It got my attention, so I asked him what would take it away. Without hesitation, he said, "God." It was as simple as that. Then he went back to his lunch.

He was so right. Only God, in His time, is going to change this terrible situation. Our problem is that we lack patience. We want this virus gone now. We need to remember what scripture tells us in 2 Peter 3:8–9, "But do not forget this one thing, dear friends: With the Lord a day is like a thousand years, and a thousand years are like a day. The Lord is not slow in keeping His promises, as some understand slowness. Instead, He is patient with you, not wanting anyone to perish, but everyone to come to repentance" (NIV).

When things are rolling along smoothly, we think we can handle life all by ourselves. But then a trial hits. Cancer is diagnosed, or a dear loved one dies. Things like broken relationships, families torn apart by drugs and alcohol, or this pandemic happen. The list goes on of things totally out of our control. Unfortunately, that's when we finally realize God is the only one truly in control, and we need Him.

With this present COVID situation, the only hope we have, and action we can take to make a difference, is for *all* of us to get on our knees and recognize the total sovereignty of God and then surrender our will.

God is brokenhearted over our world even more that we are. The difference is He is patient and long-suffering. He is waiting for the lost to be found, for the broken to repent and be restored. He loves us that much!

So, in the meantime, Romans 12:12 tells us to "Be joyful in hope, patient in affliction, faithful in prayer" (NIV).

Oh, why do we always try to figure out or try to fix the things we were never meant to take on? He already had things planned out before we were even born. Satan loves to see us question God and worry. He loves to steel our joy in the one who has so many promises for us in scripture. Joshua 1:9 reminds us, "Have I not commanded you? Be strong and courageous. Do not be afraid; do not be discouraged, for the Lord your God will be with you wherever you go" (NIV).

My husband's favorite saying during this pandemic has been this: "Don't stop living because you are afraid of dying." God has our lives planned out right down to our last breath. This virus will not change a minute of that. He, and He alone, has control of our lives. Be cautious, but live life fully, trusting in His care. He has a perfect plan.

Heavenly Father, please help me remember that Your plan is perfect. Help me to surrender my anxious thoughts of the looming virus. Help me focus on today and what You have planned for me. Help me remember I don't have to understand or know the answer; I only have to move forward in obedience. Amen.

42

Therefore, we do not lose heart.
Though outwardly we are wasting away,
yet inwardly we are being renewed day by day.
—2 Corinthians 4:16 (NIV)

MY SIX-YEAR-OLD GRANDDAUGHTER, VIVIAN, HAD
heard talk of my upcoming birthday. She asked me, "Gramma,
how old are you going to be on your birthday?" I told her that
I was going to turn sixty. She suddenly had a look of horror on
her face, then gasped and put her hand over her mouth and said,
"Oh, Gramma, no!"

I remember that when I was young, even forty seemed old.
Oh, how my views have changed. The Bible says in Job 12:12–
13a, "Wisdom belongs to the aged, and understanding to the old.
But true wisdom and power are found in God" (NLT).

There have been a few rare times that I have longed to have my
youth back. But if I was able to make a choice between being young
again and losing the wisdom gained by living through life's tough
trials and hard circumstances, I guess I would remain sixty years old.

The Lord in His wisdom sees what is best for us. I surely would not want to go back and be the person I was before the Lord opened my eyes to see how desperately I needed Him and to see His purpose for my life.

God has chosen a life for me of redemption and overwhelming grace, love, joy, peace, and hope. He loves me the way I am but sees me through the filter of His grace. Because of that, He wants me to see others in the same way.

Psalm 40:2–3 says, "He lifted me out of the slimy pit, out of mud and mire; He set my feet on a rock and gave me a firm place to stand. He put a new song in my mouth, a hymn of praise to our God. Many will see and fear the Lord, and put their trust in Him" (NIV).

He helps me to see the broken and hurting world and to be compassionate, helping others to recognize the need for a Savior who loves them the way He does, unconditionally.

My Lord, how grateful I am that You opened my eyes to the harsh reality that I was lost and a sinner in need of Your grace. You gave me a hunger for Your Word when I asked. You offered me the gift of salvation and guided my heart to submit my life to You. Thank you, Lord. I will forever be grateful. Praise your name! Amen.

43

I will give thanks to the Lord because of His
righteousness; I will sing the praises of the
name of the Lord Most High.
—Psalm 7:17 (NIV)

THREE-YEAR-OLD CALI AND I WERE in the grocery store
one day. She is a very friendly little girl, and she enjoyed talking to
each person we came upon. When we shop, she always greets each

person with a smile and hello. Most people could not resist her sweetness, and they would stop to talk to her. On this particular day, someone asked her where she had gotten her beautiful auburn curls. She smiled and said, "Jesus gave them to me for Christmas."

Through the heart of Cali, there was the great reminder that everything we have, whether we worked hard to obtain it or it was given to us (like her curls), is a gift from the Lord. The gift of being a talented athlete, an artist, a doctor, a nurse, a veterinarian, or a serviceman, carpenter, policeman, fireman ... the list goes on ... came from God. All the things we excel at doing are ordained gifts from the Creator. Yes, they are things we work hard for, but none of it would be possible if the Lord had not blessed us with the ability.

Everything we have—our family, our friends, our homes, the food we have in our fridge—all things are gifts from Him. I remember hearing this question: if one morning you woke up, and the Lord had taken away everything except the things you thanked Him for the day before, what would you have left today?

That truly is something to think about and act on. It is a great reminder to first acknowledge where everyone in our lives and everything we have came from. Then, take time daily to not only thank the Lord but praise Him for all we have been blessed with.

I remember a friend encouraging me during one of the toughest trials of my life to even thank Him for that trial. She had scripture to back it up. First Thessalonians 5:18 says, "Give thanks in all circumstances; for this is Gods will for you in Christ Jesus" (NIV). But the verse I clung to was from James 1:2–3, where he tells us, "Consider it pure joy, my brothers and sisters whenever you face trials of many kinds, because you know that the testing of your faith produces perseverance" (NIV).

Wow. I can't imagine what my life would be today without that trial. It drew me to a deep search through the scriptures, which led to a walk with the Lord in a way that I never thought was possible. Not only did I learn to thank Him during that time, but I also have thanked Him innumerable times since then for that trial. The truth is He does bring beauty out of the ashes.

Remember, a grateful heart is a happy heart. Psalm 100:4–5 says, "Enter His gates with thanksgiving and His courts with praise; give thanks to Him and praise His name. For the Lord is good and His love endures forever; His faithfulness continues through all generations" (NIV).

Oh my Father, in my heavy, dark days of pain, You drew me close to You. Your love alone kept me from giving up on life. You held me up when I was too weak to stand on my own, and at times I felt You even had to breathe for me. Then You gently showed me that I was living my life for *me*, and that was not why I was here on the earth. Thank You for opening my eyes to show me that You had a plan and a purpose for my life, to love and serve You. Thank You for being Lord of my life. Amen.

44

Don't you know that you yourself are God's
temple and that God's Spirit dwells in your midst?
—1 Corinthians 3:16 (NIV)

WHEN CAYDEN WAS TWO, HE was such a stinker. He was
cute and loveable, but like most little ones at this age, the phrase
terrible twos fit him perfectly. If there was trouble, I knew where
to look. I was constantly consoling the ones who were in his path.

One time when he was playing with one of his three-year-
old cousins, he hit him. The victim instantly began to cry and
ran toward me for a hug to make him feel better. Cayden must
have been paying more attention to what was happening than
I thought, because a few minutes later, he came and stood in
front of me. He made sure that he had my full attention and
then smacked himself on the forehead. He began to cry very
sorrowfully and said, "Gramma, Cayden hit me." So, what could
Gramma do but pick him up, hug him, and comfort him until
he felt better?

There are times in our lives when doing the right thing seems so hard. We all know right from wrong, but sometimes we just don't have the strength to do what is right. Like a two-year-old, our sin nature seems to be much stronger than our spiritual nature.

That's when daily scripture reading and prayer build up our strength to fight our sin nature. Our good friend, who happens to be our pastor, talks about how our flesh and the spiritual nature are always at battle. He says they are like two dogs fighting. He reminds us that the one we feed the most will be the strongest and will win the battle.

David Jeremiah, who is one of my favorite speakers, told of someone who wrote this: "Two natures beat within my breast, the one is foul, the one is blessed, the one I love, the one I hate. But the one I feed will dominate"[3] (anonymous). So, what do we feed our spirit? The most powerful thing there is, the Word of God. It is described in Hebrews 4:12 as a double-edged sword.

Romans 8:6 says, "So letting your sinful nature control your mind leads to death. But letting the Spirit control your mind leads to life and peace" (NLT). We need to remember that when we have a personal relationship with our Lord, the Holy Spirit dwells in us and empowers us to battle the tough things in life.

We must read the Word of God and pray daily, feeding the spiritual nature, asking God to prepare us for the next battle, because we never know when or where it will be.

Lord, there are days when I am so weak, and I disappoint myself when I fail. But knowing that You are all-knowing and yet all loving gives me the security I need to go before You, knowing there is forgiveness waiting when I truly recognize my wrong. Thank You for your forgiveness. Amen.

45

If you, Lord, kept a record of sins, Lord, who could stand?
But with You there is forgiveness, so that we can,
with reverence, serve You.
—Psalm 130: 3–4 (NIV)

ONE DAY WHILE AT MY house, four-year-old Ella took a handful of Starbursts candy out of her pocket. Her dad had given them to her. She put them on the table in front of her as she counted them out loud. Then she said, "Look, I have eight Starbursts." She had such a big smile and was so excited. I thought I would use this moment to help her to learn adding and subtracting. So I moved four of the candies in front of me, and I asked her, "OK, if you have eight candies and I take four of them, how many Starbursts do you have now?" She smiled and gathered all eight candies back into her hand and said, "I have eight, because my dad gave them to *me*."

There is something about gifts that come from our father that makes us want to hold onto them. Like with Ella's Starbursts, even the little things are special. I have three small things in my kitchen that I see almost every day. They were inexpensive things that my father gave me. My dad passed away very unexpectedly when I was only thirty-four years old, so when I look at each thing, I feel such warmth in my heart. I treasure them because they were gifts he chose for *me* out of love.

There are so many gifts that my heavenly Father has given me that I treasure, but I am thinking now of three things that I can't imagine life without; three things that I cannot see with my eyes, but I can feel them in my heart and I need them daily. They are forgiveness, grace, and mercy. They nourish my weary soul like food and water nourish my body. Because I receive them daily, it amazes me that I still carelessly fall into sin. When I do, shame comes over me like darkness on a cloudy night. At first, I am glad for the darkness, because in shame I want to hide. It is hard to admit we are wrong. Pride takes over. But then the burden of sin becomes so overwhelming, and it is too heavy for us to bear.

When we turn to our heavenly Father in repentance, forgiveness washes over us like fresh snow covers the ground after the dreary brown days of fall. Then grace warms us, like a fuzzy, warm blanket on a cold winter night, and immediately mercy is extended and we feel renewed like the sunshine on a beautiful, warm, spring day. Once again, we are able to start living as if the darkness was never there.

When we receive these gifts and see the blessing they are to us, it is then that we see the importance of offering them to others as they are needed. They are all life changing, both when we receive them and when we give them to others. They restore broken and damaged lives, restore relationships, and rescue the lost.

They come out of His deep, unconditional love, and they are a free gift to all of us at any time. When we humbly recognize our need for them and simply ask, He is faithful to deliver.

Lord Jesus, thank You so much for the many gifts You shower over me daily. Help me never to take any of them for granted. I know they came at a high cost and that You paid the price. Amen.

46

For I am the Lord your God who takes hold your
right hand and says to you, Do not fear; I will help you.
—Isaiah 41:13 (NIV)

WHEN DRAKE WAS THREE YEARS old, he would raise
one hand in the air and hold on to a family member's hand with
the other as the family would gather for prayer before a meal.

As time went on, it became just a normal thing, and we didn't think much of it. That is until one day as we gathered to eat, I asked my son, "Why does he not hold hands on each side of him?"

My son stopped and thought for a second, then said, "I don't know. I thought you taught him that." Then he asked Drake, "Why do you hold one hand up when we are praying?"

Very matter-of-factly, Drake said, "Because I am holding Jesus's hand."

As Psalm 73:23 says, "Yet I am always with you; you hold me by my right hand" (NIV). What an amazing, uplifting vison.

There are more than one hundred verses in the Bible about having childlike faith, so what does that mean? It means knowing God is present wherever we are. It means genuine humility, knowing and acting on the fact that we can do nothing without God's help. When we look to the Lord for His strength and His help, it brings glory to His name.

The entire chapter of Hebrews 11 is about faith and how faith is a gift from God. Then Ephesians 2:8–9 says, "For it is by grace you have been saved, through faith - and this is not from yourselves, it is a gift of God—not by works, so that no one can boast" (NIV).

That is why kids grasp it so easily. When taught about God's love for them, children have an unquestioning faith in God. Children have a natural way of finding joy; they have honesty, openness, meekness, and are humble. It's only as we get older that we want to take credit for the things that God has given us: the ability, wisdom, and strength to do His will. Pride sets in and hinders us from seeing where all that goodness comes from: God alone. So we must have faith like children.

Lord, thank You for the many times I have been humbled by the example of true faith that I have seen demonstrated through children. They have truly helped me grow closer to You. You are a kind and loving God who fulfills my every need. Amen.

47

One of those days Jesus went out to a
mountain side to pray, and spent the night praying to God.
—Luke 6:12 (NIV)

PRAYING EACH DAY WITH THE kids on the way to school
had become a habit after a few years, but I didn't realize how
important it was to the kids. One day as we drove off, we got into
a conversation and totally forgot to pray.

We got to the school, the kids all climbed out of the car, we
hugged and said our goodbyes, and the kids headed for the school.

All of a sudden Bailey, who was eight at the time, began
to franticly yell to the others, "We forgot to pray! We forgot to
pray!" The kids all turned around and ran back to the car. We
all stood in a circle, there in the parking lot, arms linked and
heads bowed, and we prayed. With a sigh of relief, we all said
our goodbyes again.

I drove home in awe of how that simple thing had come to
mean so much more than I could ever realize.

The New Testament records Jesus going off by Himself to pray many times. Mark 1:35 says, "Very early in the morning, while it was still dark, Jesus got up, left the house and went off to a solitary place, where He prayed" (NIV). Prayer is mentioned in the Bible more than six hundred times. Jesus Himself was recorded praying thirty-five times.

So if it was important for Jesus to pray and spend time with His Father, how much more vital is it for us to turn daily to our heavenly Father and pray? In prayers, we seek His guidance and His will for each new day. It is our loving communication with God our Father, who knows us better than anyone else does and loves us more than we can ever begin to know.

We are offered a relationship with the one who created the universe. All we have to do is call out to Him, anytime, anywhere. Wow, what a gift!

Father, help me to never take for granted this relationship with You. Soften my heart so that whenever I come before You, I may totally surrender my life and live in reverence to You. You overwhelm my heart each time I come into Your presence. You truly are my lifeline.

48

I keep my eyes always on the Lord. With
Him at my right hand, I will not be shaken.
—Psalm 16:8 (NIV)

OUR YOUNGEST GRANDCHILD, REID, WAS three
months old. As I sat feeding him his bottle, he held onto my
finger very tightly, looked up into my eyes, and I could see how
he trusted me. I was there to take care of his every need, and I
treasured every moment.

He is the eleventh grandchild the Lord has blessed us with,
and it amazes me how much love I have for each and every one
of them. I believe this is a glimpse of what our heavenly Father
feels for us. The love just poured out from me. It is love that is
overwhelming and forever. Even at fussy times, I love them just
the same.

This helpless little one was dependent on me while in my
care. I was there for his every need. Later, I laid him on the floor
for some tummy time. His little head was wobbling. He was
struggling; he wanted so badly to roll over. It was so hard to not

reach out and help him, but I know he can only gain the strength he needs if he does it on his own.

I kept him from hurting himself, but I knew this was how he would learn. Yet when I saw he couldn't go on any more, I reached down and picked him up and held him close until I knew he was ready for another challenge.

I can't help thinking how much I am like that tiny baby; I hold onto my Lord very tightly. I look to Him for all my needs, and like baby Reid was dependent on me, I am absolutely helpless without the Lord.

He poured His love out for each of us on the cross, and no matter what we do, He will never stop loving us.

We, too, go through struggles. He lovingly guides our path with the scriptures, but He knows we need to push through the tough times to get stronger. Trials are important so that we grow stronger, but He is there to pick us up and to hold and comfort us in our deep times of need.

Psalm 25:4–5 says, "Show me Your ways, Lord, teach me Your paths. Guide me in Your truth and teach me, for You are God my Savior, and my hope is in You all day long" (NIV).

Lord, I thank You for the privilege of caring for these little ones. Please give me the wisdom, strength, and discernment I need to fulfill the task You have laid out before me. Help me to always count it all joy. Amen.

49

Praise the Lord.
Blessed are those who fear the Lord,
who find great delight in His commands.
—Psalm112:1 (NIV)

MY DAUGHTER AND HER HUSBAND have always been dog lovers. So when their girls were old enough, they felt it would be a good way for them to learn responsibility by helping with the care the family's dog. Gerty was a Labrador retriever mix; they had gotten her as a puppy, and she was still young and in training, but so were the girls. Lexy was eight, and Grace was six. Their father had given them the job to take the dog outside. They have a home out in the country with a big yard, so there was no need for a leash, and the puppy already knew her boundaries. The girls watched as their dog romped and played, sniffing everything in the yard.

When it was time to go back inside, for some reason, Gerty was not listening as she should have. Of course, like all puppies, it is usually no problem to get them to go out, but most times, they do not want to go back in.

That was the case that morning. Lexy kept calling and calling her name, but there was no response from Gerty; she was ignoring Lexy completely. After several tries, Grace told Lexy, "She's not listening because you don't have enough command in your mouth."

Well, Grace sort of had the right idea.

When we think of someone giving a command, it usually is for the best of all involved. Commands are followed when the one giving the command has spent the time bonding and growing a relationship of trust and respect.

Our Master is worthy of not only trust and respect but also praise, honor, and glory.

We have a Master who loves us. He is our Father in heaven who showed us His love when He sent His Son to earth on our behalf because of our disobedience. Jesus showed us His love when He willingly responded to the Father's will, suffering on the cross by taking our punishment in restitution for our sins. Then, after His return to heaven, He sent the Holy Spirit, who lives in us, to help direct and guide our lives. That is undeniably love at its greatest.

Our part in this is to respond to our Master's commands. In the book of Matthew alone, as I read through the red letters of Jesus's words, I began to realize there are numerous commands. Beginning in chapter 4, Jesus tells us, "We must feed on every word of God."

Then He continues with commands all the way through the book of Matthew. He commands us to turn from our sin and turn to God. Jesus says: follow Him; do not worry; be a light in the world; love your enemies; help those in need; give generously; pray and fast for God's glory alone, not yours; don't store up treasures on earth; serve God alone; don't judge; be merciful; pray for the Lord to send more workers for the harvest; don't be afraid; put aside selfish ambitions; take up your cross; forgive; do not commit adultery; keep the commandments; and the list goes on.

In Ephesians 5, there is a life- and marriage-changing command: "Husbands, love your wives" (verse 5), and "the wife must respect her husband" (verse 33) (NIV). There are no exceptions in either of these commands! Nowhere does it say they have to deserve love or respect. But they are powerful when followed. God alone knows what is best for all of us. Our lives will not only be changed, but we will be blessed when we do our best to obey.

There are more than six hundred commands in the Old Testament and well over one thousand in the New Testament; each is written not to make life difficult but to make it easier and more fulfilling for us.

We know we will all fail at times, but that's where the promise of never-ending compassion and mercies poured out daily because of His deep love for us come in.

The definition of *mercy* from the *Dictionary of Oxford Languages* tells us that mercy is "compassion or forgiveness shown toward someone whom it is within ones power to punish or harm."[4] Our God certainly has that ability and right but chooses to redeem and restore. That's love.

In John 14:15, Jesus says, "If you love me, keep my commands" (NIV). *If* you love me. That is how we are to show our love for our Lord and Master, by keeping His commands.

Oh Father, how I hunger for Your will in my life, yet every day, I fail in one way or another. I am so grateful for Your grace and mercies to start fresh and new each day. I could not carry the heaviness of the burden if it were not lifted from me each day when I come to You. You are an amazing God and worthy of all my praise. In the precious name of Jesus, I pray. Amen.

50

This is the day that the Lord has made.
We will rejoice and be glad in it.
—Psalm 118:24 (NLT)

WE WERE AT THE CABIN last fall for our annual work bee. The kids love to join in with helping with the chores. It makes the jobs seem like fun and go a lot faster when everyone helps out. After the work was done, the kids found many things to do. They enjoyed riding the four-wheelers and building forts. Unfortunately, Cayden, six years old at the time, had an accident. He smashed his hand pretty severely, and he was very lucky not to have any broken bones. It was badly cut and bruised, and it required many bandages. It was evident he was in a lot of pain.

It was slow in healing, but about a week later, he was visiting, and I asked how his hand was doing. He had a big smile on his face and very excitedly told me, "I'm down to two Band-Aids a day, Gramma!" He proudly held it up for me to see.

What a great attitude! Instead of wallowing in self-pity for the pain he was still having, he found something to be thankful for. Life is so much easier when we choose to find a blessing in every situation.

Making it a habit to express thankfulness and appreciation in all parts of our lives makes us a lot more pleasant to be around. If we concentrate on what we have instead of what we don't have, we can view life with a grateful heart.

We need to have an attitude of gratitude. Psalm 9:1 says, "I will give thanks to You, Lord, with all my heart; I will tell of all Your wonderful deeds" (NIV). And Psalm 106:1 says, "Praise the Lord. Give thanks to the Lord, for He is good; His love endures forever" (NIV). Praising the Lord helps us keep our thoughts positive.

Scripture reminds us of this: "Finally, brothers and sisters, whatever is true, whatever is noble, whatever is right, whatever is pure, whatever is lovely, whatever is admirable—if anything is excellent or praiseworthy—think about such things." That's what Philippians 4:8 (NIV) tells us: think positive like Cayden does.

I have a good friend Paula who has a saying: "There will be no more stinkin' thinkin'."

Heavenly Father, I know there are many days that I don't have a thankful heart. Holy Spirit, please open my eyes to see clearly, so that I can change my attitude. I know that a thankful attitude not only pleases You, Father, but it's also an example for all those I come in contact with. I know it makes my life better as well. Amen.

51

The Lord detests lying lips,
but He delights in people who are trustworthy.
—Proverbs 12:22 (NIV)

ELLA AND CALEB WERE BORN five months apart, and they are buddies. They love to play together. One day when they were four years old, I had some hard-boiled eggs for the kids for breakfast.

Ella was eating an egg and trying to talk Caleb, who had never eaten a boiled egg before, into tasting one. He would have nothing to do with them—he said they smelled bad—but she would not give up. Stretching the truth quite a bit, she told him sometimes there are chicks in them. That didn't work. He wrinkled up his noise and said, "Eew," so she tried a different angle. "Well, I really think you would like them. Sometimes they taste like strawberries."

How easily words slip out of our mouths sometimes. As the saying goes, "Oh what a tangled web we weave, when first we practice to deceive."[5] Who really ever wants to be fooled or tricked into believing a lie?

According to 1 Peter 5, we know that there is an enemy who prowls around like a roaring lion, looking for his next victim with the most cunning deception imaginable.

Satan wants us to believe lies that cause hopelessness, and once we're discouraged, he wants our faith to be shaken. However, in any situation in our lives, we have hope in the one who wants what is best for us. Our faith in Christ is renewed when we read His Word. Psalm 33:18 says, "But the eyes of the Lord are on those who fear Him, on those whose hope is in His unfailing love" (NIV).

Satan wants us to feel defeated and afraid, but we know Isaiah 41:10 says, "Do not fear, for I am with you; do not be dismayed, for I am your God. I will strengthen you and help you; I will uphold you with my righteous right hand" (NIV). The Lord is by our side in every trial we walk through. He will not abandon us no matter what we do.

I believe the biggest lie Satan wants us to believe is that we are unloved. Really, what greater love is there than the love of a Savior who died for us?

The truth is "His love endures forever" (Psalm 136:1 NIV). He has written our life story. The Lord knows our past, our present, and our future. He knows our weaknesses and our strengths. He also knows our needs, and He is ready to supply them at just the right moment, not too early and never too late. We will never be defeated when we belong to Him. We have been redeemed, restored, and reconciled to the one who gave us life, because of His deep, deep love for us.

With the world the way it is today, so broken and divided, words are twisted to fit people's agendas. The truth as we knew it in the past has become watered down and is actually hard to find. But I have good news: there is a place where we know we can find the written truth. Taking time to read the Bible will help us recognize truth from the enemy's lies. Without a doubt, every word is completely truthful in God's Word, the Bible.

Oh Lord my God, please open my eyes and make me aware of the enemy's lies. We know he is cunning, but we also know he can be defeated when we keep our eyes on You.

52

If you remain in Me and My words remain in you,
ask whatever you wish, and it will be done for you.
—John 15:7 (NIV)

CALEB IS HOMESCHOOLED, SO HIS mom is his teacher.
One day at age seven, he was having a very hard time sitting still
and concentrating on doing his work. He was doing somersaults
and flips. He had to be called back to the tasks at hand several
times that day.

Mom was very frustrated, and she told his dad at supper of the
"not so good day" they had had at school. Dad was upset and had
a talk with Caleb, letting him know that tomorrow things would
be better or there would be severe consequences.

Surprisingly enough, the next day was great. He paid attention,
sat quietly, and did every bit of his work very well. His mom was
thrilled but a bit confused.

So she asked him what had happened to bring about such
a difference in his behavior from the day before. He thought
for a moment and then said, "Well, I guess God was watching

yesterday, and He said, 'Looks like this kid is going to need a lot of help tomorrow,' so He sent help."

That's the faith of a child. How much easier life would be if we truly trusted that the Lord's help would come if we would just ask? He truly wants us to call on Him for everything. He knows what is best. That is what Psalm 91:15 is: a promise from God to be with us in our times of trouble, and He says He will deliver us.

What our heavenly Father wants is for us to recognize our need for Him and to accept the fact that we really are not in control of our destinies.

We need to be sincere when we go before Him, humble, with heartfelt repentance, open enough to let Him overwhelm us with His unconditional love. We live in a world where we have everything at our fingertips. If we want something, Amazon can have it in our hands the next day. We can go through a drive-up window and get any food, any beverage, any time, exactly how we want it. We have become so self-absorbed.

We refuse to recognize that without God's hand on us, we can do nothing. But the truth is, with Him, we have everything. Every breath, every move we make is ordained by God. Jesus said in John 15:5, "Apart from Me you can do nothing" (NIV).

I can't image life without Jesus, and I am so glad I don't have to. He is my refuge, my comforter, and my strength.

Oh Lord, thank You for calming my heart and truly changing my life, helping me to recognize the reality that I am not in control of my life. I am grateful to finally let go and surrender, letting You guide me in the right path for Your name's sake. Amen.

53

Whoever can be trusted with very little
can also be trusted with much, and whoever is
dishonest with very little will also be dishonest with much.
—Luke 16:10 (NIV)

AT SIXTEEN, COLTON DECIDED TO try out for our high school tennis team. His favorite sport is football, but he wanted to try something new. His mom and dad kept us informed that he actually was doing very well. We hadn't been able to see him or our granddaughter Bailey play at all. I know tennis really is not a sport for a crowd of spectators, but I was glad when I finally got to see them both play.

One afternoon, I had the opportunity to go to the tennis meet. Colton played doubles with a senior who had played all four years, so it was pretty intimidating, and he worried about letting his teammate down since it was his first year.

This particular day, they were short on officials, so the players had to make their own calls. It was a pretty tight competition, and they seemed evenly matched. Colton and his teammate had a good record. With the exception of one tie, they had won all their matches. The pressure was on.

At one point, they were behind in the match. The opponent served the ball, and as it was coming down, Colton called the ball as going out of bounds. But as the ball hit, it was clear to his mom and me that the ball had come down inside the line.

After making the call, he hit the ball anyway because he realized it was in. The other team responded to his hard-hit ball, and this time, the ball did go out of bounds.

We were sitting where we had a very good view and had actually seen the other team make two bad calls. It was hard to sit quietly when that happened. I held my breath to see how it would play out.

My heart swelled. I was grateful to hear Colton speak up and tell the opponent that he had made a mistake on his call, and he felt they should replay that point. It was truly the best part of the game. He realized that ill-gotten gain is no gain at all.

Sometimes there is a cost to telling the truth, but our gain is always greater. We can have a clear conscience when we show integrity, and gain trust and respect from others. The cost of telling a lie is innumerable. First of all, it is very seldom a single lie. Usually, telling one lie leads to several more. More times than not, the truth is found out. But even if no one here on earth knows, the Lord knows, and it is very unsettling to our hearts.

A man can be poor by the world's standard of earthly belongings, but if he is honest and upright, he has integrity, and all who know him look up to him. But someone who has gained all the earthly riches one could ever want but gets no respect because they cannot be trusted has really gained nothing of true value.

John 8:32 says, "Then you will know the truth, and the truth will set you free" (NIV). This scripture tells us that even though the truth is sometimes hard, it sets us free. We don't have the burden of a lie that can be so hard to keep inside. When we strive to live a life speaking truth, we live in God's will. We bring God glory, and we experience peace of mind.

Oh Father, please give me strength to speak truth in every situation in my life. Your Word says if we ask for wisdom, You will not hold it back from us. Help me to discern truth from lies when I am faced with making decisions in my life, especially when they affect others. Thank you, Father. Amen.

54

The soothing tongue is a tree of life,
but a perverse tongue crushes the spirit.
—Proverbs 15:4 (NIV)

AFTER SCHOOL STARTED ONE FALL, it was pretty quiet at Gramma's house. The six cousins who were usually here every day were all at school. So the youngest of our grandchildren, two-year-old Drake, and I would spend time on the four-wheeler back behind my house. We would take my son's two dogs and my dog, and we would let them run in front of us for some exercise. We had a favorite route that we normally took, but it was such a beautiful day that we changed our course for a longer ride.

While we were riding, we went by a great big rock that stands about five feet tall and has a large, flat surface. I began to tell him that I had spent many hours over the years sitting on that very same rock, talking to the Lord. As the words came out of my mouth, the thought that came to me was, *He is only two years old. He doesn't comprehend what you are telling him.*

Several weeks later, we were again on one of our rides. I decided to take the long trail again. I was totally in shock because as we drove by the big rock, he waved his hand and franticly yelled, "Stop, stop! There is the rock where you always talk to God!" Wow, I couldn't believe he remembered. I guess my words did not fall on deaf ears.

It goes to show how words spoken can be one of two things: they can be something that blesses a heart or breaks it. We never know how our words will affect another person.

The words we speak can be kind, loving, encouraging, and even life changing. Those words are treasured and are something to hold onto. They are like a precious jewel; we want to keep them close to us so we can remember how they made us feel when they were first spoken. In Proverbs 16:24, scripture tells us, "Kind words are a honeycomb, sweet to the soul and healing to the bones" (NIV).

Unfortunately, there are words that are harsh, sarcastic, and hurtful, words that condemn and crush. They are like stones that are thrown. They are very painful, causing wounds that sometimes take forever to heal. As we trust in the Word of God and live by it, the cycle can be broken when we begin repaying evil with good. We choose to use our words of healing.

We are told in Proverbs 18:4, "A person's words can be life giving water; words of true wisdom are as refreshing as a bubbling brook" (NIV). There are broken, hurting people everywhere you go. We don't have to look too far or long to find them. We can be the healing balm to mend a broken heart, with just a bit of loving-kindness to those who God sends into our paths each and every day. I believe we can change the world one person at a time, by making the choice to bring comfort and healing with our words.

Lord, forgive me for the many times my words were harsh and unkind. Forgive me for the sarcasm that only made matters worse in situations. I know I can never take those words back. Please help me to make my words a blessing; help me to build and not destroy. Bring words of compassion and healing to my mind even when I myself am hurting. Lord, please bring words of restoration. Amen.

Note: The prayer rock has become a favorite place for not only my grandchildren and me but also for our neighborhood kids. There are very few days in the spring, summer, and fall that someone doesn't ask to make the trip to the prayer rock and spend time with the Lord.

55

Greet each other with Christian love.
—2 Corinthians 13:12 (NIV)

AFTER A SERIOUS SURGERY, MY six-week recovery seemed like forever. I didn't get to see my grandkids nearly enough. Then finally eight of them were over visiting after school one day. They came to help out with little jobs that needed to be done. My granddaughter Ella, eleven years old at the time, couldn't wait to share with everyone what she had learned that day while doing a report in school. The subject she had chosen was hugs.

She began to tell us that a hug is actually healing to our body because it builds up and unleashes chemicals that truly do speed up recovery. When embracing, oxytocin is released from the brain that will heal us from feelings of loneliness and anger. She said it also increases the production of dopamine levels in the brain, and that makes you happier. Hugs also release endorphins, which relieve pain and keep your heart healthier by slowing down your heart rate. Hugs stimulate the thymus gland, which regulates the production of white blood cells, and their job is to fight disease and keep you healthy.

She had come up with a plan to help Gramma with her recovery. The kids were all were pretty excited to know that they actually could help out in my healing process. So, after some discussion, they all lined up and took turns giving me hugs. They would hug me and get back in line.

After a couple of times around, one of the kids headed for the snacks I had laid out for them. Caleb, ten at the time, saw him skip out and called to his cousin, saying, "Where are you going? Come back in line! The more hugs we give Gramma, the faster she will get better, and the faster she gets better, the quicker we get to go sledding."

OK, so they did have a bit of an ulterior motive. But their hugs were warm, loving, healing, and well received.

God created the amazingly intricate human body. Psalm 139:14 says, "I praise You because I am fearfully and wonderfully made; Your works are wonderful, I know that full well" (NIV). Who could ever doubt that we have a Creator? I don't believe we will ever understand completely how intricately our bodies have been made. In Ephesians 2:10, Paul reminds us, "For we are God's handiwork, created in Christ Jesus to do good works, which God has prepared in advance for us to do" (NIV). Believe it or not, part of the plan the Lord has for us is hugging. There are more than fifty verses in the Bible about embracing and greeting with a kiss.

There is a physical disorder called touch starvation. The research is being done because of the recent pandemic. Touch starvation can lead to depression, stress, and anxiety. I see why part of Satan's scheme with the COVID virus was about trying to undermine God's healing method of hugs. Hugs are comforting and heartwarming. But now some people are so afraid of germs they refrain from any physical touching at all. That breaks my heart because the truth is physical touch is imperative to our health, both emotionally and physically.

It has been proven that babies cannot develop properly without hugs and touch. Research shows children are healthier, happier, and even smarter when they are hugged and held.

Who would ever think that an act of kindness and love could produce so much good and that a hug could be so powerful? So if you are feeling under the weather, hug someone. You will receive as much as you give.

My Lord Jesus, thank You for the blessing of loving family and friends. Help me never to take that for granted. But above all, I am grateful for the love You pour out on me. Help me to be aware of those who are around me who are lonely and need comfort and a hug from a friend. Amen.

56

Remember, O Lord, Your tender mercies
and Your loving kindnesses, for they are from of old.
—Psalm 25:6 (NKJV)

WHEN CALI WAS FOUR, SHE and I were digging potatoes in
my garden one day. I always love when the kids help me. I would
dig the shovel into the ground, and as the potatoes emerged from
the dirt, Cali would get excited. She would pick them up and
talk sweetly to each one as she would put them into the bucket.

At one point, I dug up two potatoes, a large one and one that
was very tiny. She put the large one into the bucket, and as she
picked up the small one, she held it very gently and said, "Oh
look, isn't she cute. I'm going to put her right next to her mom."
Then she gently laid it in the bucket next to the big potato. How
tenderhearted and full of love she was … for potatoes.

If a child can show love like that for a potato, can you imagine
the great, tender love the Lord has for us? He loves each one of
us individually. We are all unique. He has numbered the hairs on
our heads. He knew us in our mother's womb, and no matter what

we do today or tomorrow or what we have done in the past, He will never stop loving us with His incredible, unconditional love.

Psalm 36:5–7 says, "Your love, Lord, reaches to the heavens, Your faithfulness to the skies. Your righteousness is like the highest mountains, Your justice like the great deep. You, Lord, preserve both people and animals. How priceless is Your unfailing love, Oh God! People take refuge in the shadow of your wings" (NIV).

We cannot compare human love with God's love, because there are no conditions to God's love. He doesn't wait for us to change. He loves us even when we are unlovable. He sees us as we could be, but yet He loves us as we are. Nothing we ever do can separate us from God's love.

Romans 8:38–39 tell us, "For I am convinced that neither death nor life, neither angels nor demons, neither the present nor the future, nor any powers, neither height nor depth, nor anything else in all creation, will be able to separate us from the love of God that is in Christ Jesus our Lord" (NIV).

Lord, I have no words but thank You!

57

My dear children, I write this to you so that
you will not sin. But if anyone does sin,
we have an advocate with the Father—
Jesus Christ, the Righteous One.
—1 John 2:1 (NIV)

WHEN COLTON AND BAILEY WERE in preschool, they
were four years old and excited about going to school and riding
the bus every day. Mom and Dad would send them off to school
in the morning, go to work, and I would pick them up at eleven
o'clock.

About the third week of school, I was busy in the kitchen
when I received a phone call. The secretary from the school said
I needed to come to school immediately. Glancing at the clock, I
realized school was just starting. I quickly dressed Ella, who was
only a year old, and headed for the school.

The woman who had called from the office did not know
what was happening; she had just relayed the message from their
teacher. I was a little nervous about the reason for the call, but

when I got to the school and saw the two of them, I knew exactly why I had been summoned that morning. They were both covered from head to toe with a rainbow of colors. Their little faces showed not only the bright multicolors but also the evidence of knowing they had done something wrong. I had to restrain myself from smiling. I knew they needed to know what they had done was wrong. Evidently, the seat on the bus that they had sat on was also freshly coated with new colors as well. I knew I had to keep a serious look on my face.

Then Miss Denise, their teacher, explained to me that the children had each been asked to bring an ingredient for a recipe they were going to make in class that day. Yes, you guessed it. Their part was to bring the food coloring.

They were very sorry they had made such a mess, and we had a good talk on our way home about what happens when we make bad choices. They promised they would never do anything like that again. They truly learned their lesson and were very sad when they had to miss that day at school because it took a long time to scrub them from top to bottom. It took several days of bathing before the color finally disappeared, so for a while there was a constant reminder of their bad choices.

The truth is we all make bad choices at times. But the good news is that when we recognize our mistakes and truly repent, turning to the Lord in deep sorrow over messes that we make, it doesn't remain evident on our faces or take any time at all to be cleansed of the filth. The Bible says in Isaiah 1:18, "Come now, let us settle the matter, says the Lord. Though your sins are like scarlet, they shall be white as snow; though they are red as crimson, they shall be like wool" (NIV).

We read in Psalm 103:8–10, "The Lord is compassionate and gracious, slow to anger, abounding in love. He will not always accuse, nor will He harbor His anger forever; He does not treat us as our sins deserve or repay us according to our iniquities" (NIV).

That is worth repeating. He does not treat us as our sins deserve! He does not repay us accordingly to our actions when we repent. He loves us and wants what is best for us: restoration. So when we truly love someone, imitating Christ's love, we too should want what is best for them as well. We need to forgive and let go of the offense. That means we never bring it up again.

Psalm 103:11–12 states, "For as high as the heavens are above the earth, so great is His love for those who fear Him; as far as the east is from the west, so far has He removed our transgressions from us" (NIV).

It's that instantaneous, gone forever. In fact, the Lord doesn't want us to dwell on our sins, but He does want us to dwell on our forgiveness. You see, God chooses to forgive. Forgiveness is a choice. That's the difference. When I think about that, it overwhelms my heart and brings me to tears.

Oh Lord, I can't imagine what my life would have been like without Your forgiveness. The heaviness of my sin would be more than I could ever bear. Your love is powerful and uplifting. I know You want what is best for me, and because of that, I surrender my life to You, Lord, and I lay down my right to hold onto unforgiveness, because You have never withheld forgiveness from me. In You, Lord, I trust. Amen.

58

Blessed are those who find wisdom,
those who gain understanding.
—Proverbs 3:13 (NIV)

I HAD COLTON, WHO WAS eight years old, Cayden, four years old, and one-year-old Cali at the house for the day. We had some fun things planned, but I had a few chores I needed to attend to first.

We had eaten breakfast together, and then while I was cleaning up, Colton asked if he could go outside. It was one of the first days above zero in several weeks. Winter had set in, and it had taken a toll on all of us. Everyone was ready to get out for some fresh air, but Mom had told me as she was leaving that she didn't want him outside, because he hadn't felt good that morning. So Gramma had to abide by Mom's wishes. Not to mention he had only tennis shoes and no snow pants, and we had at least a foot of snow in the yard. He begged several times, telling me he had something he had to do out there. I continued to tell him that his mom didn't want him outside. I felt bad because it really was a beautiful day.

He finally gave up, or so I thought. Later in the morning, I went down to do some laundry in the basement. As I came back upstairs, I noticed that his shoes and jacket were both gone. I looked out the window and spotted him in the woods.

I was very upset, to say the least. I wasn't sure how to deal with this. He had deliberately disobeyed both his mom and me. My first instinct was to go to the back door and tell him to get back inside the house. But I felt God calming my angry heart, so I went into my bedroom to talk to the Lord, begging Him for help in how to deal with this situation with Colton.

After a few minutes in prayer, I got dressed and went outside. He had his back to me as I walked up to him, and he was bent down doing something. He was so engrossed in his project he didn't notice me coming. When I got close enough for him to hear me, I said, "Colton, I have a problem, and I need your help."

He turned and looked at me with a concerned look on his face. He asked me, "What do you need, Gramma?" Then he suddenly picked something up off the ground and held it up for me to see. It was a cross he had made out of two branches, and he had tied them together with bark that he had peeled off another branch. He was beaming with excitement as he handed it to me and said, "Gramma, I made this for you."

He told me that he had been thinking about making it all morning and explained how he had cut each piece. My heart just melted. I hugged him and told him I loved it. I had tears running down my cheeks.

I almost missed this huge blessing. Oh, how grateful I was that I listened to that still, small voice and turned to the Lord for wisdom instead of reacting in anger. I would have crushed his beautiful spirit. Proverbs 15:1 says, "A gentle answer turns away wrath, but a harsh word stirs up anger" (NIV).

It was a paradigm shift. When we get that one small piece of information, everything changes. Colton knows I love the Lord, and he loved me and wanted so badly to make the cross for me. I did get an opportunity later to talk about disobedience, but it was not in anger, and he felt bad that he had disobeyed.

Afterward, I wondered how many situations would have turned out differently, and how many blessings had I missed in my life, simply because I didn't ask for the Lord's wisdom in a situation. Scripture is so rich and full of life-changing information. Luke 6:31 tells us this: "Do to others as you would have them do to you" (NIV). We are to be the hands and feet of Christ here on earth.

Oh Father, please forgive me of the many times I acted out of anger without seeking Your wisdom. Help me to always look to You for guidance in tough situations. Thank You for the times in my life when I am at a loss for words, and You bring to my mind exactly what I should say and do. I can't imagine life without knowing You. You are my rock and my comfort. Amen.

59

Open my eyes that I may see the
wonderful things in Your law.
—Psalm 119:18 (NIV)

ONE DAY WHEN CALEB WAS five, he was standing in front
of the mirror and spotted some marks on his arm that caught his
attention. He stood there studying them for a long time, moving
his arm into different positions, back and forth. His mom was
beginning to wonder what was up. Suddenly, he started yelling
everyone's names: "Hey, Mom, Dad, Lexy, Grace, everybody,
come quick and see! Look! My tattoo is starting to come in! I
wonder what it will be!"

When we are young, there are so many things in life that we
think are going to appear out of nowhere: a new bike, a home, a
car, relationships, a college degree. The list goes on. But we all
know most things in life come at a cost and take a lot of time,
effort, and hard work.

I was a lot like Caleb in my early Christian years. One thing
I always admired in many other Christians was their ability to

know scriptures and be able to live scripture out in their lives so well. They seemed to have an answer from the Bible for every situation in life. I really wanted that for myself. I knew that the Word of God would help me have a much more meaningful and fulfilled life. But the truth was I didn't take the time or make the effort to really study the Bible. Oh, I would sit down now and then in the morning to read scripture, and I went to Sunday school every Sunday, and I even attended a weekly Bible study. But the truth was I had no deep hunger or desire to know more. I thought one day I would suddenly know everything in the Bible that I needed to know. It just didn't happen that way.

I was at a point in my life where I had a trial before me. At that time, I found the scripture verse in Psalm 34:18, "The Lord is close to the broken hearted: He saves those whose are crushed in spirit" (NIV). I knew that reading the Word of God would bring me closer to Him, so I started digging deeper into the Bible. I actually prayed that the Lord would give me a deep hunger for the Word, and He answered that prayer.

One day, in Psalm 119:18 I read, "Open my eyes that I may see wonderful things in your law" (NIV). That was what I wanted. I wanted to understand and hold onto God's Word, to use it to make my way through life, holding onto what I knew was powerful, life-changing truth.

After a short time, I realized that the penetration of God's Word was so powerful it was stripping away all the hardness that had accumulated around my heart.

I want to be like Paul and really live for Christ. In Galatians 2:20a, he says, "I have been crucified with Christ and I no longer live, but Christ lives within me" (NIV). I realized I needed to die to self in order to have the abundant life Jesus talks about, and it is not a one-and-done deal. It is dying to self on a daily basis.

God's Word helped me become familiar with very valuable, life-altering information. It is a rule book and playbook for life.

In it, we find the rules on how to live our lives, following in the footsteps of Jesus, and play out our lives with a Godly purpose.

Father, how grateful I am that You answer our prayers when we seek You. Thank You for Your Word and how You brought it to life before me. I know Your Word is powerful and true; it is alive and active. I cling to you, Lord. Amen.

60

The Lord bless you and keep you;
the Lord make His face to shine upon you
and be gracious to you;
the Lord turn His face toward you and give you peace.
—Numbers 6:24–26 (NIV)

AS A MOTHER OF FIVE kids and now all the grandchildren,
one thing I have learned is that when they are being too quiet,
you better check to see what is going on.

This past summer, I was blessed to have eleven-year-old
Vivian, eight-year-old Cali, Drake, who is now five, and his
two-year-old brother, Reid, spend a lot of time here. However,
they can make some huge messes at times. Through all the years
of having children in my home, I can honestly say every one of
them has loved making forts in the house. At times, every pillow
is stripped from the beds, blankets are hung everywhere, and the
cushions come off the couch. They are always trying to make it
bigger and better than the day before. Sometimes they get a little
carried away.

On this particular day, they were all up in my second story. It has two spare bedrooms, which now have been turned into a huge doll house for their American dolls. Drake and Reid are usually the pets.

It was way too quiet. I could only imagine the mess I would find, so I went upstairs to check on them. But as I reached the top of the stairs, I was pleasantly surprised when I saw the scene in front of me.

Vivian and Cali were sitting in the two rocking chairs on one side of the room, and Drake, Reid, and several dolls were sitting on the little kids' chairs that had been lined up like a classroom.

The girls were the Sunday school teachers, and both had Bibles in their laps. They were reading Bible stories to the class. That vision was a beautiful gift to me, an unexpected blessing.

I have come to realize that, in life, the Lord does send blessings along the way daily. They come in all shapes and sizes. We don't always recognize all things as blessings right away, but when we view things through the eyes of the Lord, He helps us see good in things we may not see otherwise.

I know I need to take the time to reflect and hold on tightly to each one of them. As you can see, I write them down in a journal so I will never forget them. I realize how each blessing comes with a valuable lesson.

There are two times in the book of Luke that tell us of Mary, the mother of our Lord, treasuring up things and pondering them in her heart: once, after the shepherds came to worship Jesus at His birth, when she saw her son through their eyes; and then again when Jesus was twelve years old and the family was making the long journey back from the yearly pilgrimage to Jerusalem, where Jesus lingered behind.

When they realized He was not with them, Mary and Joseph were franticly searching for Him. They found Him sitting among the teachers, who were astonished by Him in the temple courts (Luke 2:19, 51). As parents, they had to be worried sick when they couldn't find Jesus, but His mother dwelled only on the good, and the Bible tells us she clung to those precious moments. There is a reason our Lord put those two stories in scripture.

We know that even on our worst day, we can find a blessing. It all starts with our attitude. If we look at a situation with a woe-is-me attitude, we will only see the negative. But if we look for good in every situation, we will find the unexpected blessings the Lord has placed before us.

Oh Lord, thank You for the many times You pulled me out of my negative thinking. You opened my eyes to see good instead of dwelling on the bad. I know I can't change the past, but I can change my attitude and make the best of what comes my way in the future. Help me to know that because I have You in my life, I don't have to face anything alone. I praise Your name. Amen.

61

Before I formed you in the womb,
I knew you.
—Jeremiah 1:5 (NIV)

THERE ARE THREE GRANDCHILDREN I have not yet
written about, but they are held as dear in my heart as the others. I
have not had the privilege to hold them or see them yet. They were
all here on earth so briefly in their mamma's wombs and in their
daddy's hearts, but they touched our whole family in the short time
they were here. Love like that happens in an instant and goes on
forever. I know without a doubt that we will meet them in God's
perfect timing in heaven. I do long for that day. In Matthew 19:14,
Jesus said, "Let the little children come to me, and do not hinder
them, for the kingdom of heaven belongs to such as these" (NIV).

Father, You have a plan and a purpose for each life that You
create—each life. I was so blessed by reading the words in the
book of Matthew where You tell us that You have taught children
and infants to sing praises. Oh, how that warms my heart. I, too,
praise Your holy name. Amen.

For more information, please contact:
jeanniekatherinemag@gmail.com

Endnotes

1 "We Are One in the Spirit" ("They'll Know We Are Christians by Our Love") by Peter Scholtes, *The Faith We Sing*, 2223.

2 "What Child Is This?" by William Chatterton Dix, 1865.

3 "Two-Natures" ~ anonymous.

4 Definitions from *Oxford Languages*, Google.

5 "Oh, what a tangled web we weave, when first we practice to deceive!" from the poem "Marmion" by Sir Walter Scott, 1808.

Printed in the United States
by Baker & Taylor Publisher Services